MICHAEL
KEENE

SEEKERS

AFTER

TRUTH

Hinduism

Buddhism

Sikhism

CAMBRIDGE
UNIVERSITY PRESS

Published by the Press Syndicate of the University of Cambridge
The Pitt Building, Trumpington Street, Cambridge CB2 1RP
40 West 20th Street, New York, NY 10011-4211, USA
10 Stamford Road, Oakleigh, Victoria 3166, Australia

© Cambridge University Press 1993
First published 1993
Printed in Great Britain at the University Press, Cambridge
A catalogue record for this book is available from the British Library

ISBN 0 521 38626 8 paperback

Project editors: Elizabeth Paren and Gill Stacey
Picture research: Angela Anderson
Cover and interior design by Design / Section
Map illustrations by Lorraine Harrison

ACKNOWLEDGEMENTS

The publishers would like to thank the following for their
permission to include copyright photographs: Andes Press
Agency/Carlos Reyes, pp. 95, 109, 136, 156; Barnaby's Picture
Library, pp. 13, 42 (Richard Gardner), 53 (M. Lavender), 66 (Gerald
Clyde), 79 (Gerald Clyde), 96, 105 (Sarah Thorley), 153 (Richard
Gardner); Coloursport, p. 72; Chris Fairclough Colour Library,
pp. 14, 45, 118, 154; Hutchison, pp. 139, 144, 150; Christine Osborne,
pp. 77, 84, 90, 142; Panos Pictures, pp. 33, 54, 86, 100, 103, 146; Ann
& Bury Peerless, pp. 21, 22, 26, 34, 46, 62, 92, 106; Rex Features,
pp. 31, 57; David Rose, pp. 61, 71, 125, 126, 135, 149, 159; Royal
Geographical Society/Jimmy Holmes, pp. 16, 40, 81; Harjinder
Sagoo, p. 111; Peter Sanders, pp. 37, 130; Touchstone, p. 39; Geoff
Ward, p. 114; Westhill College/Enrique Berrios, p. 88; Jerry
Wooldridge, pp. 7, 8, 49, 51, 58.

CONTENTS

Part 1 Hinduism

Part 2 Buddhism

Part 3   Sikhism

HINDUISM

1. THE ORIGINS OF HINDUISM

1.1 What is Hinduism?

Focusing questions

- How many Hindus are there in the world and where are they mainly to be found?
- What is the origin of the word 'Hindu'?
- How did Hinduism spread throughout the world?

Hinduism is not only the world's oldest living faith but with some 550,000,000 members it is also the third largest religion in the modern world, after Christianity and Islam. The origins of Hinduism are somewhat obscure but it appears to have developed around 2000 **BCE** in the country where 70 per cent of Hindus are still to be found – India. Indeed, out of a total population of about 750,000,000 people, India has 450,000,000 Hindus. The remainder is made up of Muslims, Sikhs, Christians, Jews, Buddhists and members of other smaller religions. This means that some 80 per cent of the Indian population are Hindus. In neighbouring Nepal, moreover, over 90 per cent of the population are followers of the Hindu faith.

The word 'Hindu'

The word 'Hindu' comes from the pronunciation which Persian settlers gave to the word Siddhu – the ancient name for the river now know as the Indus. In time the name came to refer not just to the river, but to the whole country, and eventually to its main religion.

At that time the people of India did not have a single word to refer to their beliefs. Their sacred books simply speak of followers of the eternal law or **Dharma**. For most Hindus their faith is mainly a religious way of life based upon their sacred laws and duties.

Hinduism spreads

From India Hinduism spread, in about 1000 **CE**, along the various trade routes to the lands of the east. In most of the earliest countries to come under Hindu influence other religions such as Islam and Buddhism later became much more important, though the influence of Hinduism still remains strong in such countries as Thailand and Malaysia.

There are also sizeable Hindu communities in many Western countries such as Canada, the USA and Britain. Many of the Hindus in these countries are the descendants of early immigrants while others arrived in the 1950s and the 1960s. Many large towns in Britain now have at least one Hindu temple. There has also been a steady trickle of Western converts to Hinduism. They appreciate the quest for inner peace and contentment which is at the heart of the Hindu religion.

Key question Where did Hinduism originate and how did it spread throughout the world?

Work to do

1. India is a huge country covering some 3,250,000 square kilometres. Carry out some research of your own to discover some of the differences between people living in one part of the country and those living in another. In particular comment on:

    (a) their different languages;
    (b) their different ways of dressing;
    (c) their different ways of farming;
    (d) their different ways of worshipping.

2. What do you think the following facts about Hinduism tell you about Hinduism as a living faith?

    (a) It is about 4,000 years old.
    (b) It has over 500,000,000 followers throughout the world.
    (c) Its followers can be found in many countries.

3. Choose either the Caribbean or North America and find out when and why the first Hindu immigrants arrived there.

Key words   **BCE:** before Christian Era
                  CE: Christian Era
                  Dharma: a word which has a variety of meanings in Hindu writings, including 'righteousness', 'duty', 'way of life'

Worshippers outside a Hindu temple in India

1.2 Where did Hinduism come from?

Focusing questions

- In what way is Hinduism different from almost all of the other major world religions?
- What contribution did the Aryans make to Hinduism?
- What was the Bhakti movement?

It is not easy to pinpoint just when, or how, Hinduism began. Unlike Christianity, Islam, Buddhism and Sikhism its beginnings cannot be traced back to the teachings of a single founder. Instead, it is based upon the teachings and practices of many religious thinkers who lived at different times. Nor is there a single holy book like the Bible or the Qur'an. There are many holy books dating from different periods in Hindu history.

The Indus Valley

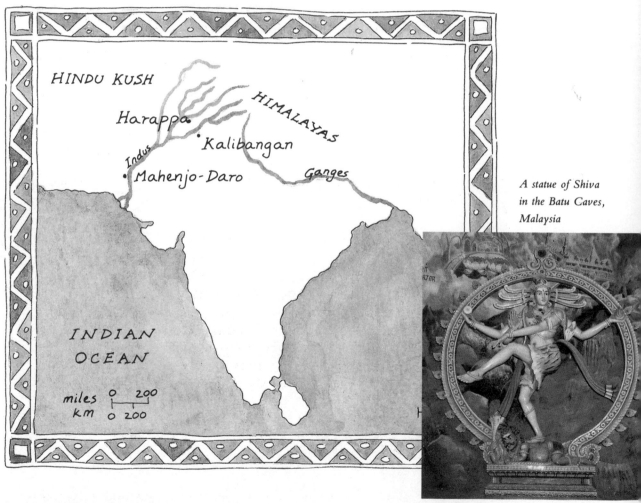

A statue of Shiva in the Batu Caves, Malaysia

Looking for the roots

The roots of Hinduism can be found in the Indus Valley civilisation which grew up around the banks of the River Indus in about 2000 BCE. This civilisation appears to have been as advanced as the better-known Egyptian and Mesopotamian civilisations which flourished around the same time. The people of the region built extensive houses and towns and produced a highly glazed form of pottery.

Although we know little of the religious beliefs and practices of the Indus Valley people, statues have been found there which give us clues. The many statues of a 'Mother Goddess' suggest that there was a strong emphasis upon fertility. One figure, a man sitting cross-legged and surrounded by animals, may well be an early form of the Hindu god, **Shiva**.

The Aryans

The prosperity of the Indus Valley began to decline in about 1500 BCE as a new group of people moved into India. They were the Aryans (the 'noble people'). These people moved about India as nomads but eventually they settled down and built their great cities in the heart of northern India, along the River Ganges. To begin with, the Aryans sacrificed animals to their gods but as they intermarried with the people from the Indus Valley their religions mingled as well, and they abandoned this practice. The Aryans provided the Hindus with their earliest collection of writings or hymns – the **Rig-Veda**. Later, around 600 BCE, another very important collection of writings, the **Upanishads**, were composed.

This emerging religion spread to southern India. The religious teachers there preferred to speak of a loving rather than an abstract God. Hymns were written about the love that existed between the gods and their worshippers. This response became known as the **Bhakti** movement.

By 400 BCE Hinduism had taken in all essential respects the form it has today.

India is a vast country. One of the reasons why Hinduism has survived for so long is its willingness to allow many people and beliefs to shelter under its umbrella. It allows and encourages each man and woman to seek the truth in their own way and at their own pace. In this it is very different from other world religions.

Key question **How did the religion which is known as Hinduism come into being?**

Work to do

1. Look at the picture of the Hindu god Shiva. You can find more information about Shiva in 3.1.

   (a) What is Shiva doing? What is another name for this god?

   (b) How many arms does Shiva have? Try to find out why.

   (c) What is under Shiva's foot? Try to find out why.

   (d) Find out the significance of the circle of flame which surrounds Shiva.

2. See if you can find more information about:

   (a) the Indus Valley civilisation;

   (b) the Aryans.

Key words **Bhakti:** literally 'love' or 'devotion'; this way of approaching God is particularly stressed in the *Bhagavad Gita* (see 2.3)

Rig-Veda: the most sacred and ancient of the many Hindu holy writings (see 2.2); rig means praise, veda means knowledge

Shiva: one of the greatest of the Hindu gods; sometimes called 'Lord of the Dance' (see 3.1)

Upanishads: important collection of Hindu writings dating from between 800 and 300 BCE (see 2.2)

1.3 The caste system

Focusing questions
- What is the caste system?
- What are the four different main castes and on what basis is the population divided up further into sub-castes?
- Who were the untouchables and what attitude did Mahatma Gandhi have towards them?

The **caste system** has been a very important part of Hinduism since its origins 4,000 years ago. It was introduced by the Aryans when they settled in north-west India. The origins of the system can be found in the holy books of the Aryans, the Vedas, which tell the myth of Purusha.

Purusha

This myth tells the story of how Brahma, the Creator-God, made the first man, Purusha. Later Purusha was sacrificed and from his body four different groups or castes were taken:

- ☐ The highest caste (the Brahmins or priests) came from the mouth. Members of this caste must keep themselves pure since they handle the sacred objects and approach the gods in worship.
- ☐ The warriors or rulers (the Kshatriyas) came from the arms.
- ☐ The skilled workers and traders (the Vaisyas) came from the thighs.
- ☐ The unskilled labourers and servants (the Shudras) came from the feet.

Outside these four castes (called 'varna') is a fifth group, traditionally known as the untouchables, who did (and often still do) the most menial and unpleasant work in Indian society. The great Indian leader, **Mahatma Gandhi**, took up the cause of the untouchables and called them the 'harijans' or 'children of God'.

The caste system in operation

In the large cities of India the caste system has been slowly breaking down during this century. The different castes are now free to mix socially and to eat together. In 1950 it became illegal for anyone to be treated as an untouchable and Hindu temples were declared open for anyone, whatever their caste, to use for worship. Educational and vocational opportunities were also extended to the lower groups in society.

Yet, in many of the villages and country areas of India, the caste system still operates. Every Hindu shares their caste group with their parents and this means that they tend to go into certain occupations. There are sub-castes for potters, builders and carpenters, for example, as there are for hundreds of different occupations. Even in the towns and amongst Hindus living abroad the choice of a marriage partner is still a matter of caste above everything else.

Key question What is the caste system and what part does it play in Hindu life?

Work to do

1. The clues in this crossword can all be answered with words used in this section. Copy the completed crossword into your books:

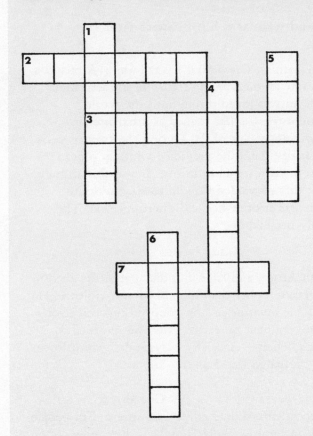

1 The artisan caste
2 The Hindu Creator-God
3 The lowest caste
4 The top caste
5 Class or group
6 The Hindu reformer
7 Another word for 'caste'

2. Why do you think the idea of the caste system first developed in India? Do you know of any other country which divides people into separate categories?

3. Try to find out how the caste system operates in India today.

Key words **caste system:** the division of Hindu society into separate classes of people
Mahatma Gandhi: Hindu reformer who took up the cause of the untouchables (see 1.4)

1.4 Mahatma Gandhi

Focusing questions

- What novel teaching did Mahatma Gandhi bring to his fight for independence and freedom in South Africa and India?
- Who were the harijans?
- How successful was Gandhi and what was his ultimate fate?

The man who came to be called Mahatma ('Great Soul') was born as Mohandas Gandhi on 2 October 1869. He became an outstanding figure in modern India and a famous religious personality who was loved throughout the world.

Born the son of a government minister, Gandhi trained as a barrister in England before going to South Africa at the age of 24. During the twenty years he lived there Gandhi experienced at first hand the prejudice white European settlers held against black people (both Africans and Indians). It was this attitude and the treatment that went with it that persuaded Gandhi to stay in South Africa in order to take up the fight against prejudice and discrimination. The method he chose to use was a highly original one.

Non-violence

As a leader of the struggles in South Africa, and later in India against the British, Gandhi stressed peaceful non-cooperation rather than bloodshed and violence. He believed that the 'peaceful and infallible doctrine of non-cooperation' was strong enough 'to paralyse the mightiest government on earth'. After he returned to India Gandhi drew on ancient Indian beliefs – especially 'satyagraha' (truth force) and 'ahimsa' (non-violence) for his campaign (see 3.5).

Call for independence

Believing that the demand for independence should come from the Indian people themselves Gandhi involved himself in local issues. He fought to help poor peasants and then joined striking textile workers. He encouraged the people to burn all of their clothes made with imported cloth and to spin their own cloth instead. Homespun cloth (khadi) became the symbol of the self-sufficiency that Gandhi hoped to develop in the Indian people. To show this, Gandhi abandoned the Western suits that he had worn as a lawyer and he began to wear the hand-woven 'dhoti', the dress of the poor Indian peasant.

Tolerance

Gandhi had very firm ideas about the kind of India that he wanted to see after the British left. Although he was a Hindu he wanted a country in which all religions could be practised freely.

In the new India he wanted to see an end to the Hindu caste system and, in particular, the state of untouchability. He called untouchability 'a blot on the Hindu religion' and he, and his fellow workers, travelled throughout India trying to remove it. He also coined a new word for those who were untouchables – he called them 'harijans' – 'children of God'.

The death of Gandhi

At midnight on 14 August 1947 India finally won her fight for freedom through using Gandhi's two principles – truth and non-violence. Less than six months later this apostle of non-violence was dead. He was shot as he stood for prayers.

India's Prime Minister, Jawaharlal Nehru, said of him:

> *The light that shone in this country was no ordinary light. It will illumine this country for many more years, and a thousand years later it will still be seen in this country.'*

Key question **Why was Mahatma Gandhi such an outstanding leader in modern India?**

Gandhi read a portion each day from the ***Bhagavad Gita***. He once said:

> *Man's ultimate aim is the realisation of God, and all his activities, political, social and religious, have to be guided by the ultimate aim of the vision of God . . . If I could persuade myself that I should find Him in a Himalayan cave I would proceed there immediately. But I know that I cannot find Him apart from humanity.*

☐ What principle does Gandhi say should direct all of the political, social and religious activities of man?

☐ Where does Gandhi believe that God is found and how did Gandhi work out this belief in his life?

Work to do
Gandhi was convinced that the best way to solve all national and international problems was through non-violence. He rejected the idea that the end justified the means, arguing that only 'pure' means could achieve great ends.

(a) What do you think he meant?

(b) Can you give *two* examples from the recent news to illustrate your answer?

Key words   ***Bhagavad Gita:*** literally, 'song of the blessed one'; the most famous and popular of all the Hindu scriptures

Mahatma Gandhi spinning cloth

1.5 Hinduism in Britain

Focusing questions
- What reasons did Hindus have to come to Britain in the 1950s?
- Which is the focal point of Hindu worship – the temple or the home?
- What are some of the differences for Hindus between living in Britain and living in India?

About 350,000 Hindus live in Britain. Most of them arrived originally as immigrants from the Indian states of Gujurat and the Punjab. A sizeable number, however, have come over the years from East Africa – especially from Kenya and Uganda. Although a few Hindus migrated to Britain before the First World War the great influx took place in the 1950s when the British government encouraged immigration to solve a shortage of labour. The policy was revised in the 1960s, however, when immigration to Britain was virtually halted.

Hindu communities in Britain

When most Hindu immigrants arrived in Britain they went to the areas where jobs were available. That was mainly in large towns, such as London, Leicester, Birmingham and Bristol, where the largest Hindu communities are today. Some Hindus, however, have moved to other parts of the country to live.

During the 1950s workers from India were mainly recruited to work in textile mills, factories and hospitals and on public transport. Many Hindus continue to work in these areas of employment but others have opened up small businesses and shops, or have trained to become doctors, solicitors, teachers or other professionals.

In many large towns temples have been opened to cater for the social and religious needs of Hindus. There are now about 40 such temples in Britain. A few temples are purpose-built but the majority are either converted churches or private houses. Although these temples are of great importance to the Hindu community, Hindus are under no obligation to attend a place of worship regularly. In practice, many Hindus only travel to their nearest temple when a special festival is being celebrated.

It is the home rather than the temple which safeguards the distinctive Hindu way of life and its religion. In every such home a 'shrine room' or corner of a room is set aside for the worship of the family's deity. This area is tended by the women of the house, who place a statue or a picture of the deity there.

The Hindu community in Britain celebrates collectively the major Hindu festivals, such as Diwali and Holi, although such celebrations can hardly match the colour and splendour of those held in India. The **rites of passage** are also kept by Hindus in Britain and children are often sent to the temple to practise their native language and their religious beliefs.

Hindu life in Britain

To a certain extent Hindus have adapted and changed their customs to fit in with the British way of life:

☐ Hindu communities in Britain do not apply the caste system as rigidly as they might do in India. For most British Hindus caste is only an important matter when it comes to choosing a marriage partner.

☐ In Western countries young Hindus are often less inclined to support an 'extended family' arrangement by which all generations of a family live together. Extended families often break down as children leave home in search of work or further education.

Hindus do not go out of their way to make new converts to their religion. There has been, nevertheless, a steady trickle of Western people who have become interested in the teachings of this ancient religion. Often those who are interested join a Hindu group under the control of a guru or spiritual teacher.

Key question **What caused many Hindus to settle in Britain and how have they maintained their way of life and religious traditions?**

Work to do

1. The photograph opposite shows a Hindu temple in Britain.
   (a) What do you notice about the way the temple is decorated?
   (b) What do you notice about the seating arrangements?

2. Is there a Hindu temple in your area? If so, try to arrange a visit. Make up some questions to ask. Here are some to start your list:
   (a) How many Hindus are there living in the area round the temple?
   (b) Was the building put up for the purpose or was it converted from some previous use? If it was originally used for something else were there any major problems in converting it for Hindu use?
   (c) Who looks after the temple? Are there any full-time officials? If so, what do they do? If not, who looks after the statues and other sacred objects?
   (d) What happens during a regular act of Hindu worship?

Key words **rites of passage:** those ceremonies which are carried out at the most important times in a person's life – birth, onset of adulthood, marriage and death

2. SACRED HINDU WRITINGS

2.1 Sruti and smriti

Focusing questions

- How were the stories of the gods and heroes of Hinduism kept alive before they were written down?
- What is sruti?
- What is smriti?

Listening to religious stories

There is an extensive range of sacred writings in Hinduism. They are used in worship – both at home and in the temple – as well as being used by Hindus in their own personal devotions. The sacred scriptures also play an important part in the celebrations at festival times and are used on all special occasions such as the sacred thread ceremony (see 5.3), marriage and at death. Hindus teach them to their children and scenes from them are often dramatised.

These sacred scriptures were all handed down by word of mouth for a considerable time before they were first written down. The text was recorded in **Sanskrit**, the classical language of India, which is still used by Hindu scholars today. Hindus believe that their scriptures fulfil two essential functions:

☐ They answer all ultimate questions about God and man. Without them, for instance, we would be in ignorance about our soul (the **atman**) and its continual reincarnation.

16

☐ They contain answers to all the practical questions about everyday living. So, for example, the scriptures teach that all forms of life are sacred and that no form of life should be killed. This means the vast majority of Hindus are vegetarian.

The sacred scriptures are divided into two categories.

Sruti

The sruti are 'those that have been heard'. This refers to those writings which are believed to have come directly from God. The priests who passed them on by word of mouth for centuries trace them back to men who heard them directly from God himself. The religion of the Aryans was based on the four Vedas (Rig, Sama, Yajur and Atharva), and later works known as the Brahmanas and the Upanishads.

Smitri

The smitri are 'those that can be remembered'. Scriptures which fall into this category are those which are human recollections of God's message to mankind. They were put together between 200 BCE and 200 CE. These scriptures are not respected so highly as those which belong in the sruti group. They include the *Mahabharata*, the *Bhagavad Gita* (the most sacred part of the *Mahabharata*), the *Ramayana*, the *Laws of Manu* and the *Puranas*.

Key question **What are the most important things that Hindus learn from their holy scriptures?**

Work to do

1. In the earliest times the sacred stories and legends of Hinduism were kept alive and passed around by word of mouth before they were written down. Can you think of *two* advantages and *two* disadvantages of keeping material alive in this way for a long time?

2. Copy this passage into your books and fill in the missing words:

Long before they were written down, the Hindu scriptures were passed on by _____ of _____. Eventually they were written down in the _____ language. All of these scriptures fall into one of two groups.

The scriptures which came directly from _____ were the _____ – 'those which had been _____'.

The scriptures which depended upon human _____ were the _____ – 'those that can be _____'. They were put together between _____ and 200 CE. These are not _____ as highly as those in the sruti group.

Key words **atman:** the soul, self or principle of life in Hindu belief
Sanskrit: the ancient language of Aryan India

2.2 The Vedas

Focusing questions
- Where did the material in the Vedas come from originally?
- What is the most important part of the Vedas and what does it contain?
- What are the Upanishads?

Most of the major world religions have just one book that is considered to be more holy, and more important, than any others. Hinduism, however, is different. It has many holy books which recount its myths, beliefs and religious practices. The oldest collection of such writings is known as the Vedas.

The origin and content of the Vedas

Although the four sections that make up the Vedas are the oldest examples of religious writing in existence they were not put together in written form for a long time. Originally the hymns and teachings found in the Vedas were passed on by word of mouth from generation to generation. They did not reach a written form until the 15th century BCE.

The Rig-Veda (see 1.2) is the most important book in the Vedas, although there is also the Sama Veda, the Yajur Veda and a later Veda, the Atharva. In all there are over 1,000 hymns in the Rig-Veda which are offered in praise of 33 different gods. These hymns are arranged in ten **mandales** and each mandale has many **mantras**. Like the other material in the Vedas the Rig-Veda is written in Sanskrit – the sacred language of the Hindus.

The Upanishads

Some Hindus chose to follow teachers who encouraged them to meditate and reflect. Some of these teachings were brought together in the Upanishads ('sitting near' or 'close by'), which were written between 600 and 200 BCE. Although there are many such writings only a few of them, some 13 in all, have been accepted as important.

The gods who are central in the Vedas are not so prominent in the Upanishads. These are concerned with the relationship between the individual soul (the atman) and the 'One Soul of the Universe' (**Brahman**). The aim of each person is set out as the merging of the individual soul with the One Universal soul. When this happens a person is released from the round of birth, life and death and achieves 'moksha' (release). You can find two quotations from the Upanishads in this section.

Using the Vedas in worship

Although the visitor to a Hindu temple is likely to find a copy of the Vedas, the book itself is rarely used in public worship. Verses and hymns taken from the Vedas and the Upanishads are used as the backbone of public worship.

Key question What is the oldest collection of Hindu writings and what does it contain?

Two quotations from the Vedas

What sin we have ever committed against an intimate, O Varuna, against a friend or a companion at any time, a brother, a neighbour, or a stranger, free us from it, O Varuna.

If like gamblers at play we have cheated, whether in truth or without knowing, free us from our guilt, O God. So may we be dear to thee, O Varuna.

For an awakened soul Indra, Varuna, Agni, Aditya, Chandra — all these names represent only one basic power and spiritual reality.

☐ To which particular god is the first hymn addressed?
☐ What does the worshipper ask of his god?
☐ In 3.1 we will ask whether Hindus believe in one God or many. What answer does the second quotation give to that question?

Two quotations from the Upanishads

Those who do not know the field walk time and again over the treasure hidden beneath their feet and do not find it: in the same way all creatures pass through the world of Brahman day by day but do not find it for they are carried away by unreality.

From the unreal lead me to the real, from darkness lead me to light, from death lead me to immortality.

☐ Who is Brahman?
☐ What do you think the treasure is that so many people fail to find?
☐ In the prayer three things are asked for. What are they?

Work to do
Using the information that you have been given in this section define each of the following words in no more than *two* sentences:
    (a) Rig-Veda
    (b) mandale
    (c) mantra
    (d) Upanishads

Key words   **Brahman:** the holy power present in the whole of nature and throughout the universe

mandale: division of a book

mantra: sacred formula or chant which can be of help in meditation in guiding the mind along a certain path (see 4.4 for more information)

2.3 The *Mahabharata*

Focusing questions
- ■ What story is found in the *Mahabharata?*
- ■ What lessons are there to be learned from the *Mahabharata?*
- ■ What is the importance of the *Bhagavad Gita?*

The *Mahabharata* (literally 'the great story of the war of the Bharatas') is the world's longest poem and was composed, in Sanskrit, during the 9th century BCE. The story told in the poem's 200,000 verses is that of a power struggle between two families, both of whom were descended from King Bharata.

The story of the poem

King Pandu gave·up his throne so that Dhritarashtra, his brother, could rule in his place. The new king brought up Pandu's sons (the Pandavas) alongside his own (the Kauravas). After a time, however, the Kauravas became jealous of their cousins' heroism and good works, and the Pandavas decided they would be safer living in the forest, disguised as Brahmins or priests. Their cousins thought that they had died but one of the Pandavas, Arjuna, emerged from the forest, won an archery contest and with it the hand of a princess, Draupadi. So extraordinary were some of the feats performed by Arjuna that the Kauravas realised that their cousins must still be alive.

The Kauravas agreed to divide their kingdom with the Pandavas but only gave them the poorest parts. Through hard work, though, the poor part of the kingdom became the most prosperous. This increased the jealousy of the Kauravas, who challenged the eldest Pandava prince to a game of dice. The Kauravas used loaded dice (provided by an uncle) and so the Pandava prince lost all his lands, his brothers and finally his wife. He was banished to a forest for 12 years and sentenced to spend a 13th year without being recognised.

After the 13 years of exile were completed the Pandavas returned and demanded their kingdom. When this was refused both sides prepared for war. The fighting lasted for 18 days before the Kauravas were defeated. The Pandavas celebrated their victory by turning to a life of meditation in the Himalayas where they awaited death and future bliss.

The *Bhagavad Gita*

The *Bhagavad Gita* is the most sacred part of the *Mahabharata*, recording the appearance of the god **Krishna** disguised as Arjuna's charioteer. Although he is a considerable warrior Arjuna does not want to kill the friends and relatives who are part of the Kauravas' army. He says that he would rather lay down his own arms and be killed. Krishna urges Arjuna to fight and in so doing articulates many of the basic beliefs of Hinduism, including the relationship between Brahman and man and how man can reach his own personal salvation.

The value of the *Mahabharata*

The *Mahabharata* has had a very important influence on the Indian way of life throughout its 3,000 year history. It contains important wisdom, teaching, comment and advice which have been conveyed through drama, puppet theatre, dance, music and skilful story-telling. Most people, therefore, although they are very unlikely to have read the Mahabharata in full, are familiar with the outline of the story.

Key question What is the story that forms the basis of the *Mahabharata* and what influence has it had upon the Indian way of life?

In the *Bhagavad Gita*, Krishna speaks to Arjuna about the 'atman' or soul, which is indestructible and is reborn into a new body after death. He says:

> *Atman is not born and never dies. It is eternal, everlasting and ancient. It is not destroyed when the body dies. If a man knows for certain atman is constant and exists eternally, how can that man kill anyone or cause anyone's death? As a man throws away used and worn-out clothes after death to enter new ones, so does atman leave worn-out bodies after death to enter new ones.*

☐ What is atman?
☐ What does this extract say about the nature of atman?
☐ How does the picture of worn-out clothes illustrate what happens to the soul after death?

Work to do
This illustration is taken from an edition of the *Mahabharata*.

(a) Which two armies are facing each other here?
(b) Why was there a war?
(c) Who spent 13 years in exile and why?
(d) What happened in the end?
(e) What lessons do you think a Hindu might learn from reading the *Mahabharata*?

Key words **Krishna:** one of the most famous and popular of the Hindu gods, an avatar, or incarnation, of Vishnu

2.4 The *Ramayana*

Focusing questions

- What is the main theme of the *Ramayana?*
- What happened in the *Ramayana* after Rama lost his kingdom?
- How did Rama regain control of his kingdom and find his wife, Sita?
- Why did Rama abandon Sita?

The *Ramayana* is an epic poem of 24,000 two-line verses written, like the even longer *Mahabharata*, in Sanskrit. It was composed in about 1 CE and is said to be the work of one man, Valmiki. Like the *Mahabharata* it is a highly moral story showing the conflict between good and evil, right and wrong.

The story of Rama and Sita

The *Ramayana* tells the story of Prince **Rama** and his wife **Sita**. The prince is king of Ayodhya but he loses his right to reign and is forced into exile. His brother, Lakshman, and his wife, Sita, accompany him. The three exiles live in the Dandaka forest for some time until Sita is kidnapped by Ravana, the demon king. Sita is taken to the demon's island kingdom (Lanka, now Sri Lanka). When Rama and his brother discover that Sita has been kidnapped they are overcome with grief. They set off to find her but she seems to have disappeared without trace.

In their wanderings Rama and Lakshman come to a southern kingdom whose ruler, Sugriva, has been deposed by his brother. Rama agrees to help Sugriva regain his throne and, in return, the deposed king sends his monkey-general, Hanuman, to help Rama look for Sita. After searching for many days Hanuman

A scene from the Ramayana

finally tracks Sita down to Lanka and finds her being held in a palace garden, watched over by several fierce female demons.

Rama and Sugriva put together a large army, cross the sea to Lanka and attack Ravana's forces. In one of the battles Lakshman is injured, but he recovers after being treated by some herbs provided by Hanuman. In the decisive battle Rama kills Ravana, rescues Sita and returns to Ayodhya with Sita, Lakshman and Hanuman. The people welcome them home joyfully and soon make Rama their king. He rules the kingdom with great equity and fairness.

There is, however, another twist to the story. The people doubt whether Sita has been totally faithful to Rama after being away from him for so long. Their suspicions appear to be justified when she discovers that she is pregnant. Although she protests that she only loves Rama and has not been unfaithful to him, the king abandons Sita near the hermitage of Valmiki. There she gives birth to twins – Lawa and Kusha. Years later Sita goes to Ayodhya with her twins and meets Rama. She still protests her innocence and declares that the earth will open up and swallow her if she is pure. The earth does open up and she immediately disappears from view. Rama is heart-broken and looks after his two sons himself until, some years later, he hands his kingdom over to them.

The moral of the story

In this story all of the main characters highlight the immense differences that exist between good and evil. Sita is a classic example of purity, virtue and faithfulness. Lakshman is a faithful and affectionate brother. Rama is the obedient son, a faithful husband and a wise ruler. Yet, of course, the character of Rama was blemished when he placed his duty to his people above his willingness to believe his wife. He remains, however, one of the most popular Hindu gods.

This story is kept alive from generation to generation of Hindus through story-telling, shadow puppets and drama. It forms the basis of the festival of Dussehra (see 4.5), although in that festival it is the goddess, Durga, rather than Hanuman who helps Rama to find Sita.

Key question How does the story of Rama and Sita show that good finally triumphs over evil?

Work to do

1. The photograph opposite illustrates an incident from the story of Rama and Sita. Describe the part played in that story by each of the following:

(a) Rama

(b) Sita

(c) Lakshman

(d) Ravana

(e) Hanuman

2. How do you think that the story of Rama and Sita might offer encouragement to a Hindu who was finding life particularly difficult?

Key words **Rama:** hero of the epic *Ramayana* and believed to be one of the ten avatars of Vishnu

Sita: an important woman in Hindu mythology, she is held up as the ideal example of womanhood

3. GOD AND HUMAN EXISTENCE

3.1 One god or many?

Focusing questions
- Who is the impersonal 'Universal Spirit' in Hinduism?
- Which three gods together form the Trimurti?
- Which goddess can take one of two forms?

Brahman

Hindus believe that there is one world spirit, or god, eternal and everywhere. This is Brahman, who takes no human form. Hindus are free to imagine God in any form that they find helpful. The images that are such a feature of Hindu worship are simply displaying one aspect of the whole being of Brahman. The atman, or human soul, is part of Brahman and will be reabsorbed back into the World Spirit after many reincarnations.

There are three main forms that Brahman has taken.

Brahma – the Creator-God: in the old myths **Brahma** is often depicted as a royal person with four heads and riding on a goose whilst reading the Vedas. Although there are still some temples dedicated to Brahma, he is not as popular today as Shiva and **Vishnu**.

Vishnu – the preserver and maintainer of life: there are many temples in north India dedicated to Vishnu. From time to time Vishnu has come to earth as an **avatar** to reveal the truth of God. Krishna and Rama are the best-known examples of such avatars. Generally speaking Vaishnavites (those who worship Vishnu) believe that he has made nine avatars altogether, with one more, as Kalki, still to come.

Shiva – the god of life, death and rebirth: this god is the symbol of the force that both creates and destroys. He always has at least four hands to show that he has the power over life, death, good and evil. He destroys all those things which are old and unneeded. This is why he is often shown wearing a necklace of skulls. At the same time his destructive work does allow new things to happen. Shiva is usually portrayed as the Lord of the Dance, whose energy keeps the universe going. Sometimes he dances on the back of a demon, or monster. This is the demon of ignorance, which Shiva is destroying beneath his feet.

Together Brahma, Vishnu and Shiva form the **Trimurti**.

Other deities

There are millions of other deities who also reveal some part of the character of the Universal Spirit. Often the goddesses who are the wives of Shiva and Vishnu – Parvati and Lakshmi – are worshipped. Parvati is particularly interesting. She can appear in two forms. As Parvati she is peace-loving and gentle but in her other guise, as Kali, she is very fierce. Before setting out on a journey, Hindus pray to **Ganesha**, the god of wisdom and knowledge, who has the head of an elephant. Another popular god is Krishna, who is one of the appearances of Vishnu.

What different aspects of the Universal Spirit do the gods Brahma, Vishnu and Shiva show?

Work to do

1. What would be your response to the question 'Do Hindus believe in one god or many?'

2. This photograph shows a Hindu goddess who can appear in two very different forms. As Parvati she is both peace-loving and gentle. As Kali, or Durga, however, she can be very fierce and, like her husband, Shiva, often wears a necklace of skulls. Why do you think that Hinduism has a goddess who can show two violently different sides to her personality?

Diwali Greetings

Parvati and Kali as they appear on a Diwali greetings card

Key words **avatar:** any appearance of a god in human form
Brahma: Hindu Creator-God and first member of the triad with Vishnu and Shiva (see below). In sculpture he is sometimes shown as one figure with three faces
Ganesha: the son of Shiva; according to legend Shiva accidentally cut Ganesha's head off when in a temper and put an elephant's head on his son in its place
Trimurti: the triad of the three great Hindu gods – Brahma, Vishnu and Shiva
Vishnu: a benevolent god, who is concerned to preserve life

3.2 The avatars of Vishnu

Focusing questions

■ What is an avatar?
■ Which of the avatars of Vishnu have already taken place and how many are still to come?
■ What is the purpose of the avatars?

An avatar is one of a god's various earthly appearances (incarnations). The most important avatars in Hindu belief have been those of the god Vishnu. Most Hindus believe that there are ten avatars of Vishnu, the last of which is yet to take place. The clearest statement about the purpose of these avatars is found in the *Bhagavad Gita* (see extract opposite).

The manifestations of Vishnu

So far Vishnu has appeared on earth in nine different forms or guises. On each occasion the avatar was to save the earth from some great calamity.

1. He took the form of a *fish* to save the guru Manu and his sacred books from a great flood. You can read the words that the Fish spoke to Manu later in this section.
2. In the flood the gods lost a special drink, called amrita, which kept their youth and made them immortal. In the form of a giant *tortoise* Vishnu helped the gods to recover the amrita from the bottom of the ocean.
3. A demon cast the earth to the bottom of the oceans but Vishnu, in the form of a *boar*, spread it out so that it could float on the top of the waters.

4. A demon discovered a secret that made it neither man nor animal. It appeared immortal and caused great distress. To kill it Vishnu took a form that was *half man and half lion.*

5. When another demon gained control of the earth Vishnu appeared before him as a *dwarf.* The demon allowed him to have as much of the earth as he could cover in three strides. Becoming a great giant, Vishnu then covered the whole earth in three steps.

6. The warrior class (the Kshatriyas) once threatened to overthrow the priestly class (the Brahmins). Vishnu appeared as *Rama with the axe* and saved the situation.

7. *Rama, the Prince of Ayodhya* is one of Hinduism's favourite gods and his story is told, as we have seen in 2.4, in the *Ramayana.*

8. *Krishna* is Hinduism's most popular god. During his time on earth this avatar killed many demons and his wicked uncle, before ruling as a wise king.

9. This is a disputed avatar since many Hindus do not believe that Vishnu could have come as *Buddha.* Some even say that he appeared as Buddha to give mankind the wrong teaching.

At the end of the present age Vishnu will appear for the last time as *Kalki*, riding a white horse and carrying a flaming sword in his hand.

Some of the avatars of Vishnu are rarely worshipped nowadays. In some Hindu temples, though, statues of all avatars can still be found.

Key question **Vishnu appeared on earth in nine different forms. Can you explain each avatar?**

The Fish speaks to Manu – from the *Bhagavad Gita*

> *Those born of sweat, those born of eggs, or of water, and those living creatures which slough their skins – place them all on this boat and save them, for they have no protector.*

☐ Four categories of life are saved by the Fish. What are they?

Work to do

1. In this extract from the *Bhagavad Gita* Krishna is revealing that he is an avatar of Vishnu:

> *Whenever the Sacred Law fails, and evil raises its head,*
> *I take embodied birth.*
> *To guard the righteous, to root out sinners,*
> *and to establish the Sacred Law,*
> *I am born from age to age.*

(a) When does an avatar take place?
(b) What do you think the phrase 'I take embodied birth' means?
(c) What does the avatar do when he is on earth?

2. The photograph opposite shows one of Vishnu's avatars. What is an avatar, and which one is illustrated here?

3. Describe, in your own words, the work undertaken by each of the following avatars of Vishnu on their visits to earth:
   (a) the Fish; (b) the Tortoise; (c) the Boar; (d) the Man–Lion;
   (e) the Dwarf; (f) Rama; (g) Krishna; (h) Buddha.

3.3 The soul

Focusing questions
- What happens to the soul, or atman, at the end of time?
- What is Dharma?
- What is karma?
- What is moksha?

Atman

Hinduism teaches that there is a spark of God in every man and this it calls the 'atman' or soul. The soul:

- is not controlled by the body;
- is not affected by the evil actions of the body;
- does not die when the body dies.

In the end, though, the atman is reunited with the Brahman, from whom it came in the first place. When this happens it merges into the Absolute Spirit just as salt dissolves in water.

Dharma

Dharma is an individual's personal code of conduct. In Hinduism what people do is more important than what they believe. Each Hindu is expected to carry out religious duties, family responsibilities and work, according to their Dharma, by enjoying the good things of creation that the gods have provided. It is mainly through Dharma that the soul makes its way slowly towards the final liberation.

Karma

The soul, however, does have to reckon with the law of **karma**. Everyone is subject to the cosmic law of karma which determines a person's destiny. Karma is the total effect of a person's actions, whether for good or evil. Every action provides its own effect, either in this or in a future existence. All individuals must strive to their full ability to achieve a good karma since these deeds give value to life. We will look at the different paths to liberation that Hinduism holds out in the next section, but one of the most important ways of achieving a good karma is through **yoga**.

Samsara

The cycle of birth, death and rebirth which controls all human life (**samsara**) will almost certainly be long, but it is not eternal. Every atman is capable of reaching its ultimate goal – union with the Brahman. Righteous and dutiful living can open up the door to breaking the cycle of samsara and so reaching liberation.

Moksha

When the cycle of samsara is broken and the soul is liberated, the final stage of existence (**moksha**) has been reached. The journey towards liberation has been essential. In the various reincarnations the soul has travelled through the different **ashramas** and overcome the temptations of the world. Along the way material success will have been enjoyed since it is only by truly enjoying the good things of life that moksha can be finally reached.

Key question   **According to Hinduism, what is the main reason for a person's existence?**

The state of moksha is described in this conversation between Chitra and Uddalaca:

> *The soul that passes through the heavenly door arrives at the world of the gods . . . It casts away the works of good and evil . . . the soul arrives at the palace that is invincible, the abode that is beyond improvement, the throne that is supremely luminous. Here sits the Supreme Being and asks, Who art thou? He replies, What thou art, I am. Who am I? The Real? What is the Real? It embraces the universe. Thou art the universe.*

☐ What name is given in this extract to the place where the soul is truly liberated?

☐ How is this place described in the extract?

Work to do

1. Hindu philosophy is very difficult to understand and so word pictures are often used to explain very difficult ideas. The idea of Brahman being reunited with the soul (atman) has been likened to salt dissolving in water, or a drop of water merging with the ocean.

   (a) Why do you think that this is a particularly useful illustration?

   (b) Can you think of your own 'word picture' to illustrate this idea?

2. Try to explain simply, in your own words, what is meant by each of the following:

   (a) karma

   (b) moksha

   (c) samsara

Key words   **ashramas:** the four stages of life – student, householder, hermit and spiritual pilgrim (see 5.1)

karma: good deeds performed in this life which affect a person's form in the next

moksha: release from the series of rebirths

samsara: the coming again and again of the soul to birth, death and rebirth

yoga: literally a 'yoke'; a method of self-control and meditation (see also 3.4)

3.4 Paths to liberation

■ What is the path of bhakti?
■ Why is the path of knowledge the most difficult for a person to follow in the quest for liberation?
■ What is yoga and how might a Hindu use it to find liberation?

In a Hindu's daily life there are several paths along which a person is able to walk in their desire to understand and worship God. These paths also provide the means by which a person may eventually find release from the seemingly unending cycle of birth, death and rebirth.

The path of bhakti (devotion)

This is loving devotion to a personal god. This way of expressing personal faith and devotion places importance on the particular image of god that a person has chosen to worship. The domestic shrine found in every Hindu home, together with the temple, also have important parts to play in the path of bhakti. At the domestic shrine **puja** is offered as an act of devotion. Hymn singing, telling the stories of the gods, religious drama, celebrating the religious festivals and pilgrimages are all an important part of the bhakti tradition. Apart from offering daily worship at the shrine of their personal deity and serving others in its name, the worshipper also follows the path of bhakti by trying to remember the deity at all times.

The path of karma (actions)

According to the *Bhagavad Gita* the moral law of existence is that good deeds bear good fruit and bad deeds bad fruit. This acts like a chain of cause and effect since the way that a person lives in one existence affects the level at which they return in the next. Everything that a person does, including sleeping, working, eating and speaking, affects their karma. Every human being must take particular care to do only those actions which produce a good karma, as all actions affect a person's next reincarnation.

The path of jnana (knowledge)

Jnana is the most difficult path for a person to take to liberation. Not only does it require constant guidance from a spiritual teacher (a guru) but also the ability to understand all of the sacred scriptures. A few people are able to free themselves from attachment to the world through a clear understanding of the scriptures.

The path of yoga (meditation)

Yoga is a series of physical and mental exercises designed to give a person control over their mind and body. Although, in many Western societies, people simply use a form of yoga as a way to achieving better health, for Hindus it is a strict spiritual discipline. Yoga has been practised in India for thousands of years. A person who practises yoga is called a yogi (male) or a yogini (female).

The ancient Hindu books set out a number of requirements for anyone who wants to practise yoga successfully. They must practise self-control, non-violence, truthfulness, chastity and avoid greed. They must master certain postures (called 'asanas'), the most important of which is the 'lotus position'. In this position a person sits cross-legged with their feet resting on their thighs. Breathing exercises also aid concentration, as does focusing the mind on a statue of a deity or on a special diagram called a 'yantra'. Mantras can also be sung to lead the mind forward and so raise its awareness of its own oneness with the Supreme Spirit, Brahman.

Key question **What are the different paths open to Hindus in their quest for liberation?**

The Lord Krishna speaks these words in the *Bhagavad Gita*:

> *Whatever you do, eat, offer as an oblation,*
> *give as a gift or undertake as a penance,*
> *offer all that to Me, O Arjuna.*

☐ Which of the four paths to liberation is this particular quotation recommending?

Work to do
Whilst most Hindus use yoga, a person does not have to be a Hindu to do so. Invite someone into your class to show you what yoga is and to explain to you why they benefit from it.

Key words **jnana:** knowledge that comes from having a direct insight into the nature of ultimate reality
puja: act of worship or reverence offered to a person's chosen god

Practising yoga

3.5 Ahimsa

Focusing questions
- Which religions teach that no living creature should be harmed?
- What is ahimsa?
- Which Indian leader adapted the doctrine of ahimsa to put pressure on the British to leave India?

The **Buddha** (c. 560–480 BCE) was just one of many Indian teachers who taught his followers the doctrine of ahimsa. Both **Buddhism** and Hinduism, along with other Eastern religions, teach that no living creature should be harmed.

A respect for all forms of life – insects, animals, birds, fish and human beings – is an important feature of Hinduism. Ahimsa expresses the sanctity, or holiness, of all forms of life. Indeed many Hindus find it impossible to draw any real distinction between animal and human life. Some of them believe that a person can be reborn as an animal and so all forms of life must be treated with kindness and thoughtfulness.

The best-known example of this care is the respect which Hindus extend to the cow. Hindus will not kill, or eat the meat of, cows. Although not all Hindus are vegetarians, the vast majority are and the cow is given its unique status because it produces the milk and cheese which helps young and old, rich and poor, to stay healthy.

'Ahimsa' means taking no action to harm any living creature. To put the principle into practice in everyday life would mean that a person must refrain from any actions that could lead to the taking of life or the shedding of blood. The eating of any animal flesh is also to be avoided. Ideally, a person should also make sure that they do not cause any emotional or mental distress to any living thing either.

Yet ahimsa does not involve the removal or alleviation of pain or distress that is already being caused. India is a society in which poverty and malnutrition cause distress on a wide scale, in which beggars and the poor live wretched lives on the streets of Calcutta and Bombay each night and in which the caste system condemns millions of people to do miserable jobs for the whole of their lives. Hindus believe that this pain and suffering stems from the karma of a previous life and consequently nothing can be done about it. A person can only hope that they will carry forward an improved karma into the next life.

The West became particularly aware of the doctrine of ahimsa in the 1930s and the 1940s when Mahatma Gandhi used it so powerfully as a weapon to force the British to leave India. He interpreted the doctrine particularly in terms of 'non-violence' and 'non-cooperation' and the British found that they had nothing in their armoury with which to fight it (see 1.4).

Key question **What is ahimsa and how do Hindus apply the doctrine to their everyday lives? What aspects of life does ahimsa not apply to, and why?**

Mahatma Gandhi taught that all religions should be tolerant towards each other:

> *Our inward prayer should be that a Hindu should be a better Hindu, a Muslim a better Muslim and a Christian a better Christian.*

☐ What do you think the link was between Gandhi's teaching on tolerance and his strong belief in ahimsa?

Key words   **Buddha:** the Enlightened One, the founder of Buddhism
Buddhism: religion based on the teachings of Gautama Siddharta, the Buddha

*Cows are a common sight
in Indian streets*

4. HINDU WORSHIP

4.1 Worship in the home

Focusing questions
- How important is the family in Hindu society?
- What is 'puja'?
- What is the Gyatri Mantra and how often is it repeated during a day?

Most Hindu worship takes place in the home rather than in the temple. The main reason for this is that Hindu society is based on the family unit, which safeguards society's traditions and customs. The traditional Hindu family is an **extended family** and this gives to all its members a strong feeling of solidarity and identity. It is in the family that children learn the customs of their religion and the obligations that stem from the caste system. They are also brought up to observe the five daily duties:

☐ yoga and meditation;
☐ worship and reverence for the deity (god);
☐ a respect for elders and ancestors;

☐ the extending of hospitality to the needy and to holy men;
☐ a respect and kindness for all living creatures.

Puja

Puja is religious worship and can take place within the home. Usually this involves presenting offerings to the deity in the shrine-room and chanting special words called mantras. Every Hindu home has its own shrine and this is treated as a very holy place. Sometimes it is little more than a shelf on a wall, although the ideal is to have a room that can be dedicated to the family's god. Here an image, or statue, of the god is surrounded by flowers and **incense**.

Women play a very important part in the worship ceremonies that take place in the home. These begin early in the morning when the god is 'woken up' by a lighted candle that is placed in front of him or her. The statue is then washed and wiped all over with **ghee** as a sign of great respect. Special coloured powders are brushed onto the deity as well. The family sometimes chants a mantra or can meditate in silence. Of all the prayers that are used the most popular is the **Gyatri Mantra**. Brahmins repeat this three times during the day – at dawn, at midday, and at sunset. It is also used in public worship and on ceremonial occasions such as births, marriages or the opening of important buildings.

Women in Hindu homes have the responsibility of ensuring that the worship customs are performed properly, that the major religious festivals are kept and that the children learn the great stories of their culture and their religion. In other words, it is largely up to Hindu women to make sure that the traditions and customs of the faith continue unbroken from one generation to the next.

Key question **What is the importance of the home, and particularly women in the home, for keeping alive many of the religious customs and traditions of Hinduism?**

Work to do

1. In the photograph opposite you can see a Hindu family shrine in the home.
   (a) What is a Hindu act of worship called?
   (b) What are the five daily religious duties?
   (c) What can you see on the shelves of this shrine?
   (d) Whose responsibility do you think it is to maintain this shrine?
   (e) What happens in the morning before such an act of worship is carried out?
   (f) What is the Gyatri Mantra?

2. In a Hindu family cooking and washing-up are also seen as religious activities, alongside giving offerings to the shrine. How do you think such everyday activities could be described as religious?

Key words **extended family:** when more than two generations of a family live close to each other or even under the same roof
ghee: butter that has been clarified (impurities have been removed by heating)
Gyatri Mantra: most sacred verse of the Rig-Veda (see 1.2); it is repeated by Brahmins three times a day
incense: gum or spice which produces a sweet aromatic smell when it is burned

4.2 Worship in the temple

Focusing questions
- Where are Hindu temples usually built?
- What role does the priest play in public Hindu worship?
- What is the worshipper expected to do during an act of public worship?

Hindu temples are usually built at places where, according to tradition, a god has appeared or lived on earth. These manifestations or appearances of the gods are called 'avatars' (see 3.1). Some of the temples built on these sites are large, spacious and beautiful. Others, however, are scarcely large enough to contain the priest and an image of the god. It is not the size of the temple that matters but its sanctity and the attitude of the worshippers as they come to present their offering.

The form of worship

Most Hindu temples have at least one priest. He carries the important responsibility of looking after the image of the god and of helping the people to worship in an appropriate way. The people do not worship the image. They come to worship the god of whom the image is an appropriate symbol. To do this the worshippers usually arrive at the temple early in the morning and ring a bell-rope to announce their arrival for worship. They also take off their shoes as they enter the temple as a sign of respect. They present their gifts to the priest, who takes them into the shrine-room to lay them before the statue. In the larger Hindu temples the priest then offers prayers in front of the people and these are made up of three parts:

- the **bhajan**, which is the singing of special hymns;
- the **havan**, which involves offering the sacrifice of fire to the god or goddess – to do this the priest lights a small fire in front of the statue using wood and ghee;
- the **arti**, where a small tray containing five lights is waved in front of the statue of the god. It is then taken round to the people, who run their hands over the flames before wiping their hands over their heads. Hindus believe that when they do this they are receiving power from their god.

Tilak

During the worship in the temple people place a dot or stripes of a special powder on their foreheads. This is the **tilak**, which indicates that the person has been to worship. Its shape represents the god or goddess that the person has worshipped. (The tilak is not to be confused with the red dot that Hindu women place on their foreheads to show that they are married – see 5.4.)

Key question What are the main forms of worship in Hindu temples?

These words of the god Krishna are recorded in the *Bhagavad Gita*:
> Whatever a zealous soul may offer,
> Be it a leaf, a flower, fruit or water,
> That I willingly accept
> For it was given in love.

- What quality makes an offering acceptable to the deity?

Work to do

1. What are the three things that Hindu worshippers do when they first arrive at the temple?

2. This photograph shows Hindus worshipping in a temple in India.
   (a) What are some of the people holding?
   (b) What form of worship do you think is going on?
   (c) What else does the picture tell you about Hindu worship?

3. In this section several special words are used. Explain, in one or two sentences of your own:
   (a) arti
   (b) tilak
   (c) bhajan
   (d) havan

Key words **arti:** part of Hindu worship where a tray containing five lights is passed amongst the worshippers
bhajan: Hindu hymn
havan: form of worship using a fire offering
tilak: spot or stripes placed on worshippers' foreheads after they have been to worship

4.3 Food

Focusing questions
- Why are most Hindus vegetarian?
- Which animal is sacred to most Hindus and why?
- Does fasting play an important part in the Hindu religion?

Although there are few hard and fast rules in Hinduism about what believers can and cannot eat, a number of Hindu beliefs may affect a believer's diet.

Vegetarianism

A large number of Hindus are **vegetarians**. This is mainly because they believe that all life is sacred and so it is wrong to kill animals for food and most also believe it is wrong to eat eggs. There are also practical reasons for not eating meat: in India it is expensive and cannot be kept for any length of time. Protein is provided in the diet of most Hindus by lentils and other pulses and by lots of milk and milk products. There are many regional styles of cooking in India. For example, vegetables such as cauliflowers and potatoes cooked with spices and served with bread are likely to form the staple diet in the north, while in the south rice would be served instead of bread and the vegetables would be cooked differently.

The sacred cow

Although some Hindus do eat meat at least occasionally, almost all do not eat beef. Hindus hold all life to be sacred, but the cow is held in special regard. This fact is tied to the belief in 'ahimsa' – respect for the sacredness of all life (see 3.5). Often Hindus look upon the cow as a symbol of the earth itself, which gives freely but asks for very little in return. The free gifts from the cow are the milk and milk products which are essential items in the Indian diet. Butter, ghee, cheese and yoghurt are available to most villagers as long as their cows are kept alive and in good health.

Pollution and purity

The caste to which a person belongs and the demands of ritual purity also affect the food that Hindus eat. The traditional teaching of Hinduism is that a person should not accept any food, especially food that has been cooked, from a member of a lower caste.

The higher a person is in the caste system the purer he or she is thought to be. Food touched or prepared by someone in a lower caste is thought to be polluted. Brahmins are at the top of the caste system (see 1.3), many of them are cooks and their food may be eaten by anyone.

In modern Indian cities, however, this idea of 'pollution' has largely died out. Few people who dine in a restaurant are likely to worry themselves about the caste of the cook or of those who are serving the food.

Fasting

As with many other religions fasting is an important part of the Hindu religion. Many Hindus fast on certain holidays and at other times, as a religious discipline. Some devout Hindus fast for one day a week, or even more often. Others have a partial fast during which they only take liquids and certain grains.

Key question How does Hinduism affect the eating habits of those who follow it?

Work to do

1. Imagine that a Hindu who believes in vegetarianism and a member of another religion who does not are holding a conversation. What arguments do you think a Hindu might bring forward for the religious and physical benefits of adopting a vegetarian way of life? What arguments might the other person bring forward for suggesting that food does not have any particular religious significance?

2. Find out as much as you can about vegetarianism and then answer these questions:

   (a) What is vegetarianism?
   (b) Why are so many Hindus vegetarian?
   (c) What are thought to be some of the physical benefits of eating only a vegetarian diet?
   (d) Does it surprise you that thoughts of health and religious beliefs are brought together in the preference of many Hindus for following a vegetarian way of life? Explain your answer.

Key words **vegetarian:** anyone who chooses not to eat meat. Vegetarians may also refuse fish or products that derive from animals such as eggs or milk

A typical Indian vegetarian meal

4.4 Aids to worship

Focusing questions
■ What is the sacred syllable in Hinduism and what is its significance?
■ How do Hindus bring the sacred syllable into their everyday lives?
■ What is a mantra?
■ What is a mandala?

The sacred syllable

The sacred syllable of Hinduism first occurred in the holy books of the Upanishads and is made up of three sounds – A, U and M – and a humming nasal sound. Hindus take the syllable to signify:

☐ the three Vedas or holy books (2.2);
☐ the three elements or worlds of earth, atmosphere and heaven;
☐ the three gods in the Hindu Trimurti or triad – Brahma, Shiva and Vishnu. Brahma is the creator, Vishnu the preserver and Shiva the destroyer (see 3.1).

Many Hindus, though, take AUM, or OM, to represent the whole universe and its Oneness. As such it symbolises Brahman, the World or Universal Spirit. Sometimes it is simply taken to mean 'Yes' in the sense of 'Yes, there is an Eternal Spirit behind the every-changing world.'

AUM is often used as part of a mantra in worship as well as being placed at the

Hindu posters on sale in south India

beginning and end of all Hindu books. It is also uttered before any Hindu act of worship, all prayers, readings from the holy books and periods of meditation. This is because the syllable is believed to hold the key to understanding the universe.

Since AUM is the symbol of spiritual good Hindus like to have a plaque or poster of the sacred syllable somewhere in their home. Often it will be incorporated into the family shrine. It can also be found in many Hindu homes on such practical items as paperweights or lampshades. Many Hindus wear it on a pendant around their necks.

Mantras

Mantras (see 2.2) play a very important part in Hindu worship. They are words, or short phrases, which are continually repeated during meditation in order to empty the mind of unnecessary concerns. Freed in this way the mind is able to concentrate on liberation from the maya, or illusion.

In mantra yoga a guru gives each person a mantra of their own. That mantra must remain a secret since it only applies to that person. It must not be divulged to anyone else. Then, when the secret words are spoken, that person is believed to have power over objects. Some yogis are said to have moved objects simply by repeating the mantra.

Mandalas

A **mandala** is a symbolic diagram. The diagram is usually surrounded by a circle in which patterns can be made in sand, metal, stone or paper. Spaces in the mandala represent gods. Incantations are usually sung whilst a mandala is being prepared and spiritual forces are believed to descend and appear.

Key question   **Why are the sacred syllable and mantras an important part of Hindu worship and how might a worshipper make use of them?**

Work to do
Try to invite a practising Hindu into your school to speak about worship in the community to which they belong. In particular try to find out the answers to these important questions:

(a) What use do Hindus make of the sacred symbol in private and public worship?

(b) What use might be made of the sacred syllable in private life and in the home? Is it visible in their home and, if so, why?

(c) What is a mantra and how is it used?

(d) Do they sing mantras? What do they believe that a mantra accomplishes?

(e) What do the spaces in a mandala represent?

(f) Do they make use of a mandala? What meaning do they attach to it?

(g) How important is the temple in the religious life of a Hindu? How often are they expected to attend the temple for worship? Do they go regularly or only for special festivals? What is an act of worship like in a temple? Is it purely a personal act or do they worship together with other Hindus?

Key words   **mandala:** symbolic diagram which is believed to contain real psychic energy

4.5 Hindu festivals

Focusing questions

■ Which Hindu goddess is at the centre of the celebration of Durga Puja and how is she worshipped?
■ How is the theme of the triumph of good over evil brought out during Dussehra?
■ What is the main theme of the festival of Diwali?

Celebrating Diwali

There are a large number of Hindu festivals. Many, however, are confined to certain parts of India whilst others are only observed by particular groups or communities. Two festivals, though, stand out as being particularly important. The dates for both of them are determined by the ancient Hindu calendar, which has twelve months, based on the phases of the moon.

Durga Puja and Dussehra

Durga Puja is the main Hindu festival and is held in honour of the goddess **Durga**. It is also known as 'Navaratri' or 'Nine nights' since that is the length of time that it lasts. In north India this is the time when the winter crops are sown (September/October). As a symbol of this, in some areas barley is sown in a small dish on the first day of the festival and by the end it has begun to sprout.

During this important festival the people celebrate the victory of good over evil. In Bengal this takes the form of celebrating the victory of the goddess Durga over the evil buffalo demon. The goddess is represented by a many-sided image, which is paraded through the streets as the people dance. At the end of the festival statues of the goddess are made out of papier mâché and are taken to the sea to be buried beneath the waters.

In other parts of India it is the victory of the god Rama (the seventh avatar of Vishnu) over the demon god Ravana which exemplifies the Hindu belief that good will always, in the end, triumph over evil. This great story is told in the sacred *Ramayana* (see 2.4) and the story is acted out, in instalments, in many Indian villages during **Dussehra**, the day after Durga Puja. The actor playing Rama throws a lighted torch into an effigy of Ravana which has been stuffed with fireworks.

Diwali (the festival of lights)

Diwali is the Hindu New Year festival and is held in either October or November. During this time Hindus celebrate the return of their hero Rama from exile to become the rightful king (see 2.4). The word Diwali means 'row of lights' and for this festival lamps are placed in windows and on the roofs of houses to welcome Rama home, with fireworks adding to the carnival atmosphere.

The theme of light is also extended to welcome **Lakshmi**, the goddess of wealth, into Hindu homes. The woman of the house performs a Lakshmi puja to bring health, wealth and good fortune to members of her family for the year ahead. In many Hindu homes this good fortune is attracted by people playing cards or other games of chance late into the night. Also at this time Hindu business people close their account books and open new ones. They too perform a special puja to Lakshmi, hoping that she will cause their businesses to prosper in the year ahead.

Key question   **How are the two main Hindu festivals celebrated?**

Work to do

1. Carry out some research of your own to find out more about the Hindu festival of Dussehra/Durga Puja. In particular, try to discover:
   (a) how Durga defeated the demon;
   (b) which other gods are also honoured at Dussehra;
   (c) what part mata, or local goddesses, play in Dussehra;
   (d) how the festivals are celebrated in Britain.

2. There are many Hindu festivals which are not mentioned in this section. Try to find out as much as you can about *two* of them. Here is a list to help you:
   (a) festivals to commemorate the birth of Prince Rama, Hanuman, Narasimha and Lord Krishna
   (b) Ganesh Chaturthi
   (c) Mahashivaratri
   (d) Holi
   (e) Ratha Yatra
   (f) Saraswita Puja

Key words   **Durga:** Hindu goddess who was the wife or consort of Shiva. She is regarded as the outward expression of his divine energy
Durga Puja: main Hindu festival, celebrated particularly in Bengal
Dussehra: Hindu festival which celebrates the victory of Lord Rama over King Ravana of Lanka
Lakshmi: Hindu goddess of good fortune and the wife of the great god Vishnu. She is thought of as a beauty and is sometimes depicted as having four arms and holding a lotus flower

43

4.6 Hindu pilgrimages

Focusing questions
- **What are the main reasons for Hindus to make pilgrimages?**
- **What kinds of places are likely to be holy to Hindus?**
- **What are the seven holy rivers of Hinduism?**
- **Which special festivals draw large numbers of Hindu pilgrims?**

Although Hindu believers are not under any obligation to make pilgrimages, they are an important element in Hinduism. The pilgrimage may be short or long. During a religious festival the journey may only involve travelling a short distance to the shrine of a particular deity. Longer journeys are common, however, as many pilgrims travel to important cities or shrines.

Reasons for pilgrimage

There are several reasons why a Hindu might feel obliged to undertake a pilgrimage at a particular time. A person might wish:

- [ ] to gain religious merit by visiting one of Hinduism's sacred places;
- [ ] to fulfil a vow made earlier in their life;
- [ ] to bathe in the waters of a holy river – this is believed to be an important act of purification;
- [ ] to walk around a shrine at a holy place – while they do this pilgrims make sure that they keep the shrine on their right-hand side;
- [ ] to scatter the ashes of a loved relative in the waters of a holy river – this is believed to be particularly beneficial if the ashes can be scattered over the waters of the River Ganges at Benares;
- [ ] to make amends for breaking a sacred law;
- [ ] to be cured from some physical illness, although most Hindus do not believe that their holy places and shrines can offer healing of this kind.

Places of pilgrimage

There are many places of religious pilgrimage in India. They can be divided into two main groups:

- [ ] natural creations, such as rivers or mountains, which inspire feelings of reverence because of their beauty – in all there are seven holy rivers: the Indus, the Ganges (Ganga), the Godavari, the Narmada, the Jumna, the Saraswita, which runs under the ground, and the Kaveri;
- [ ] man-made structures or places that are associated with important events in Hindu history – high up on the list of important places of pilgrimage are the great temples of Hinduism.

Special festivals

Whilst pilgrims can visit the holy rivers, mountains and temples at any time, they are particularly encouraged to go at special festival times. One such festival is the Kumbh Mela, which is only held every 12 years at Benares, the place where the Rivers Ganges and Jumna meet. This draws over 2,000,000 pilgrims. The confluence of two rivers, incidentally, is considered to be a particularly holy place. Another festival which draws huge crowds is held at the **Jaganatha** temple in Puri.

Key question   Why are pilgrimages important in Hinduism?

Work to do

1. The photograph above shows pilgrims at Benares, on the River Ganges.
   (a) What does the photograph tell you about the atmosphere at this place of pilgrimage?
   (b) Why are some people immersing themselves in the water?
   (c) Give three reasons why a Hindu might undertake such a pilgrimage.
   (d) What special festival is held here once every 12 years?

2. There is a myth about the River Ganges which explains why it has been considered to be holy for centuries. Try to find out this story for yourself.

3. Try to find some of the seven holy rivers on a map of India.

Key words   **Jaganatha:** large vehicle which is used to carry Lord Jaganatha, a form of Vishnu, in a procession at the festival at Jaganatha. (This is the root of the English word 'juggernaut'.)

5. THE STAGES OF LIFE

5.1 The four stages

Focusing questions
- How many stages are there in a twice-born Hindu's life?
- What are the first two of these stages?
- What makes stages three and four different from the others?
- What ends everyone's search?

The last stage of life – the spiritual pilgrim

For male Hindus in the top three castes, the 'twice-born', the journey through life is made up of four stages, or ashramas. From childhood to old age each individual is concerned to find out the answers to the basic questions of life:

- ☐ Why am I here?
- ☐ What is life all about?
- ☐ What happens to me after I die?

Whilst no one can hope to discover more than a tiny fraction of the answers in one short lifetime, the search must go on relentlessly.

Stage one – the student

This stage begins, for members of the top three castes, when they are 'born again' and a sacred thread is placed around their necks (5.3). At the end of this ceremony the child is placed under the guidance of a guru or spiritual teacher. In the past children left home to study with their guru but now they visit him from time to time in their search for the truth. Without the guidance of the guru no one can hope to make any real spiritual progress.

Stage two – the householder

The student stage ends when a young Hindu man decides to marry and take on family responsibilities. Through bringing children into the world a Hindu is being given the opportunity to achieve three goals:

- ☐ a release from all basic human desires and energies through marriage, having children and bringing them up;
- ☐ a contribution to the well-being of society by working hard;
- ☐ the duty of carrying out whatever demands his particular caste places on him.

Stage three – retirement

When a Hindu retires from active work the circle returns to the beginning. He is expected to become a student again. Now he sets out to find answers to the two most difficult questions of all:

☐ What is the universe, and life itself, really about?
☐ How do I discover my true self?

A few Hindus give up work early to seek the answers. When their first grandchild is born a Hindu can, by tradition, leave his family and devote himself to prayer, study and **meditation**. The *Laws of Manu*, a Hindu holy book, give him the authority to do this.

Stage four – the spiritual pilgrim

Only those men who have left their family and possessions behind can enter fully into this stage. The true spiritual pilgrim must:

☐ consider his staff and his begging bowl to be his only possessions;
☐ wander from place to place without any cares or worries;
☐ eat whatever comes his way;
☐ share his wisdom with anyone that he meets.

Hinduism, then, sees the whole of life as a search. Only by searching can a man find his true self. The start of the search is the beginning of life itself. The end is moksha (see 3.3) or rebirth.

Key question **What are the four stages of life, or ashramas, through which a Hindu passes?**

The *Laws of Manu*, an ancient religious text, says:

> *When the householder sees his skin wrinkled and his hair white and the sons of his sons, then he should retire to the forest.*

☐ Why do you think that the vast majority of twice-born Hindus no longer follow this advice?

Work to do

1. Explain, in no more than two sentences, what each of these words means:
  (a) guru
  (b) ashramas
  (c) meditation

2. What do you think about dividing a person's life up into a series of stages? Do you think that the four stages of Hinduism are an accurate reflection of the stages through which most people will pass?

Key words **meditation:** technique for clearing one's mind of all earthly concerns by following special rules concerning breathing, postures and ways of thinking. This frees the mind to concentrate on God and so to reach a higher stage of spiritual awareness

5.2 Hindu birth ceremonies

Focusing questions
■ What is a samskara?
■ When do the first three samskaras take place?
■ Why are the fourth and fifth samskaras particularly important?

In Hindu tradition each ashrama, or stage in life, should last for 25 years. This means that everyone, if they live properly, should be able to look forward to reaching their 100th birthday!

The early samskaras

In the Hindu religion there are certain rituals or **samskaras** which prepare the believer for the different stages of life. There are 16 samskaras altogether: the first five of them take place before and after the birth of a baby.

The first samskara takes place even before a baby is conceived when a Hindu couple pray about the kind of baby that they would like. A second samskara takes place in the third month of pregnancy to be followed by another, five months later. The second and third samskaras will, Hindus believe, give protection to the baby and strengthen the mother.

The fourth and fifth samskaras

The fourth samskara takes place soon after the baby is born. The child is washed and then the sacred syllable (see 4.4) is written on the tongue using a golden pen dipped in honey. Another samskara is performed 11 days later when the baby receives its name. In Hinduism the choice of name is very important since it can bring good fortune on the child throughout its lifetime. In fact, at this time, the child is often given two names:

☐ the public name by which he or she will be known to others;
☐ the secret name which will only be used on special religious occasions.

The baby receives its name in a simple way. The father just leans over the baby and whispers in its ear: 'Your name is . . .'. The father than repeats a series of mantras in which he asks that strength, understanding and wisdom should be granted to his child. He also seeks protection for the child from evil spirits.

In devout Hindu families this ceremony is carried out by a priest. In most Hindu families, however, it is informally carried out in the baby's home. The baby's name is announced by the oldest woman in the family whilst the other women sing songs to the new baby. All of the married women are given a handful of cooked pulses, such as chick peas, together with light refreshments.

Key question In what different ways do the five first samskaras prepare a Hindu baby for the four stages of life?

Work to do

1. Write down this list of the first five samskaras.
   (a) Opposite each one write down the time when the ritual takes place.
   First samskara
   Second samskara
   Third samskara

Fourth samskara

Fifth samskara

(b) Can you suggest any reasons why there are two samskaras during pregnancy and why there are two so soon after the baby's birth?

2. What is the sacred syllable? Look back at section 4.4 if necessary.

3. What are the four ashramas? Try to write them down without referring to another section in this book.

Key words **samskaras:** rituals which prepare Hindus for the different stages of life. If the correct observances are undertaken at each stage then the bad effects of karma can be overcome and a better rebirth obtained

A Hindu family take their baby to the temple

5.3 The sacred thread ceremony

Focusing questions

- Who can take part in the sacred thread ceremony?
- How does a Hindu boy receive his sacred thread?
- How does a Hindu man treat his sacred thread?
- What does the spiritual knot remind the boy to do?

Of the first 11 samskaras the most important is the **sacred thread** ceremony. This is only performed on boys and is, theoretically, open to boys from the top three castes – Brahmins, Kshatriyas and Vaisyas. In practice, though, it usually only applies to children from the Brahmin caste and those born into wealthy families.

The ceremony

This ceremony can take place at any time from the age of nine onwards. Once it has taken place the child is known as 'twice-born' since he is believed to have entered into new life through the ceremony.

For the ceremony itself the priest and the child sit on opposite sides of a fire which is sacred to **Agni** as prayers and hymns are chanted. The boy then repeats prayers after the priest until a special thread is placed around his shoulder and waist. Before the ceremony ends, the boy is given his own personal mantra which he must use every time he prays.

Those who receive a sacred thread wear it for the rest of their lives. A special ceremony is held each year, though, at which the sacred thread can be changed for a new one. Often men gather on the banks of the River Ganges, bathe and then change their thread.

The 'spiritual knot'

The thread itself has three strings made of cotton or wool and dyed separately – white, red and yellow. The strands are tied together with a special knot. This is called the 'Brahma Granthi' ('spiritual knot'). It reminds the boy that he has three debts to discharge throughout his life:

- ☐ to his god for life itself and all that sustains him through it;
- ☐ to his parents for giving him life and teaching him about Hinduism;
- ☐ to his ancestors and teachers for imparting to him wisdom and knowledge.

After the ceremony

Receiving his sacred thread is a very important milestone in the life of every high-caste Hindu boy. From now on he is expected to:

- ☐ pray three times every day;
- ☐ perform the ceremonies of the puja;
- ☐ read, study and learn the sacred scriptures.

After receiving his sacred thread in the past a child was expected to wander through the countryside relying on others for his food and shelter. Now his parents simply hand him over to his new guru for spiritual instruction.

Key question Why is the sacred thread ceremony such an important milestone in the life of a young Hindu?

These are the words of the guru as he accepts responsibility for the spiritual guidance of a new pupil:

> My pupil, I accept you as one of my children. From now on your happiness and sorrow will be my happiness and sorrow. I place you in the hands of Almighty God. By His blessings may you enjoy a hundred autumns happily and merrily!

☐ Why do you think that the teacher takes on the happiness and sorrow of his pupil?

☐ What do you think the guru means when he says: 'By His blessings may you enjoy a hundred autumns happily and merrily'?

Around the sacred fire

Work to do

1. There are several mistakes in this paragraph. Copy it into your book with the mistakes corrected.

   Only boys from the top three castes are allowed to wear the sacred thread but in practice it only applies to those from the Vaisya caste. During the ceremony a fire is lit in honour of Agre, the goddess of plenty and prosperity. The boy receives his sacred thread, which has four strands, which are tied together with a special knot – the spiritual knot.

2. Do you know of any other initiation ceremonies in other religions which take place when a boy or girl is on the verge of adulthood? Do you think that they are a good idea? What useful purpose might they serve? What is the ideal age for such a ceremony?

Key words **Agni:** Hindu god of fire, believed to mediate between the gods and men. Many Hindu ceremonies centre around fire and Agni is believed to consume the offerings and carry their fragrance to the gods

sacred thread: Hindu symbol of initiation, worn by boys from the left shoulder to the right hip

5.4 Marriage

Focusing questions
- What happens at the 13th samskara?
- What must happen before a Hindu wedding can take place?
- Why does a Hindu wedding take place in front of a holy fire?
- What do the seven steps taken in the wedding service symbolise?

The 13th samskara is reached when a Hindu marries and becomes a householder. The first ashrama has been completed. Now, during the second ashrama, the Hindu sets himself three religious aims:

- to attain some religious merit in the hope that he can avoid being reborn;
- to achieve wealth;
- to enjoy pleasure.

Preparation for marriage

Most Hindu marriages are arranged by parents. In India girls are allowed to marry at the age of eighteen whilst boys have to wait another three years. Hindus living elsewhere, however, are bound by the marriage laws of the country in which they live. When choosing a suitable partner for their child Hindu parents take two factors, in particular, into account:

- Both man and woman must come from the same caste.
- Horoscopes must be drawn up for the man and woman and these will be shown to a priest to see whether the couple are compatible. These horoscopes will also enable the priest to tell the parents the best time for the wedding to take place.

The wedding clothes

A Hindu bride is prepared carefully for her wedding. **Henna** is painted on to her hands and feet. In the middle of her forehead a red spot (called a 'tilaka') is painted to show that she has been blessed by God. In India the traditional wedding outfit for a bride to wear is a red sari trimmed with gold supplemented with gold jewellery. The groom, for his part, can either wear a 'kurta-pajana' (a long, loose-fitting top with trousers) or a Western-style suit.

The wedding ceremony

The actual marriage ceremony is performed by a Brahmin priest and takes place, as do many Hindu religious ceremonies, around a fire which symbolises the presence and blessing of God. The priest keeps the fire burning throughout the ceremony by pouring ghee onto the flames. He also throws rice and spices onto the fire since these are the traditional Hindu symbols of fertility.

The bride's parents give her to the groom by placing her hand in his. A cord is then placed around the groom's neck whilst the other end is attached to the bride's sari. Together the couple take seven steps around the sacred fire as prayers are said. The steps represent: the provision of food; the need for physical strength; the acquisition of wealth; the need for good fortune; the hope of having children; the regularity of the seasons and good harvests; a lasting friendship.

Key question   What happens at a Hindu wedding ceremony?

Whilst taking the seven steps around the fire during the wedding ceremony, the man says to the woman:

With utmost love to each other may we walk together . . . May we make our minds united, of the same vows and of the same thoughts. I am the wind and you are the melody. I am the melody and you are the words.

On their last step the couple say to each other:

Into my will I take thy heart. Thy heart shall follow mine. And the heart of mine be yours.

☐ How do the couple seem to see their married life ahead?
☐ What do you think is meant by:
a 'I am the wind and you are the melody. I am the melody and you are the words.'
b 'Into my will I take thy heart.'

Work to do
It is a Hindu custom for parents to choose the marriage partners of their children.

(a) What is this custom called and what might be its main advantages and disadvantages?

(b) What might Hindu parents want to bear in mind when they are choosing a marriage partner for their child?

(c) Although Hindu marriages are arranged, tradition insists that the couple should enter their marriage freely. Why do you think that this is so important?

Key words **henna:** an orange plant dye traditionally used to decorate the bride for a Hindu wedding

The couple are tied together in this Hindu wedding

5.5 Death

Focusing questions

■ What is the final samskara?
■ Which method of disposing of a dead body do Hindus favour?
■ Who plays the leading part in a Hindu funeral and what is he expected to do?

After the 14th samskara (the third ashrama), which is retirement from work, and the 15th samskara (the fourth ashrama), which is a turning-away from all that is worldly, only one samskara remains. That is death, followed by cremation.

The funeral ceremony

Hindu tradition only allows holy men and babies to be buried. Otherwise the usual practice is for the corpse to be reduced to ashes by burning (cremation). A cremation ground is to be found outside most Indian villages, where the bodies are burnt beneath a covering of wood, usually sandalwood.

This cremation takes place on the same day as death if the person has died before sunset. As soon as the death is confirmed, the body is washed and dressed by relatives. It is then carried in a procession to the cremation ground on a stretcher, covered by a simple cloth. If possible, the dead person's eldest son leads the procession. When the place of cremation is reached he walks three times around the funeral pyre, pours holy water over the body and then puts a flame to the wood. He expresses the hopes of everyone present by saying the words that you will find in the extract opposite. A constant supply of ghee is thrown on the flames to keep them alight. Dry pieces of sugar cane are also squeezed between the splints of sandalwood.

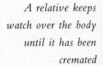

A relative keeps watch over the body until it has been cremated

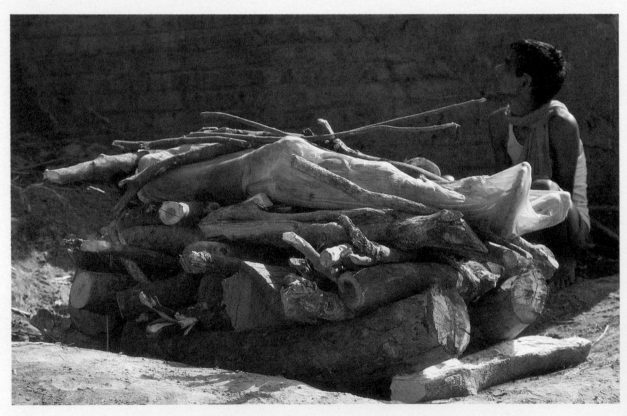

After the cremation

On the day after the cremation the eldest son, or the closest relative, collects the bones and ashes and scatters them over the waters of the nearest river. Since Hindus believe that anyone who has their ashes scattered on the waters of the Ganges escapes the cycle of birth and rebirth many relatives travel to the great river to dispose of the ashes.

The cremation is followed by ten days of important religious ceremonies during which every effort is made to ensure that the naked soul of the deceased, released from the shell of the body, finds another casing in which to live. Hindus believe that the soul is immortal, and the body simply provides a temporary home for it to live in. During the ten days of mourning:

☐ the eldest son offers rice and milk every day in case the soul of the dead person returns to trouble its family if it cannot find a new home;

☐ the relatives visit the eldest son on the fourth day to comfort his family and give them presents – they also offer up prayers for the soul of the departed;

☐ a final meeting of sympathy (a 'kriya') is held on the 11th day and this marks the time when the soul becomes free to pass into another body.

Key question   **What is the significance of the ceremonies held by a Hindu family in the days immediately following a person's death?**

Explaining rebirth the *Bhagavad Gita* says:

> *As a man puts off his worn out clothes*
> *and puts on other new ones,*
> *so the embodied soul puts off worn out bodies,*
> *and goes to others that are new.*

☐ What does the phrase 'the embodied soul' mean? What does it tell us about the Hindu belief in the relationship between the soul and body?

☐ What everyday picture is given to explain the idea of rebirth?

☐ When does the soul discard one body and take on another?

Work to do

1. These words are spoken by the eldest son as he applies the flame to the funeral pyre:

I apply fire to all the limits of the person who, willingly or unwillingly, might have committed lapses and is now under the clutches of death – a person attended with virtue and vice, greed and ignorance. May he attain the shining regions.

(a) What words does the son use to describe the shortcomings of his father?

(b) What phrase is used to describe heaven?

2. Find out how Hindus cremate people who have died in this country. If possible, invite a Hindu in to your school to give you the information and answer your questions. In particular, try to find out:

(a) if the eldest son still plays the leading role in a Hindu cremation;

(b) how the cremation is carried out;

(c) whether Hindus in this country bury their dead;

(d) what happens to the ashes after a Hindu cremation.

PART 2

BUDDHISM

6. HOW DID BUDDHISM BEGIN?

6.1 Being a Buddhist

Focusing questions

- On whose example and teachings is Buddhism based?
- On which two main teachings is Buddhism based?
- What are the 'three refuges'?
- How many Buddhists are there throughout the world?

Buddhism began with the enlightenment and teachings of one man – Siddhartha Gautama Buddha. He was an Indian prince who lived about 2,500 years ago, although the exact date of his birth is disputed. He was 'enlightened' in about 531 BCE and then became a well-known teacher, who travelled extensively to pass on the teachings that now form the basis of Buddhism. Unlike the founders of many other religions, the Buddha did not rely on miracles or the gods as the basis of his message. Instead, he encouraged people to look at their actions and consider the reasons for their behaviour. He showed them that only if they acted wisely and considerately could they live a happy and fulfilled life on earth.

Following the Buddha

Being a Buddhist means, above everything else, desiring to know, understand and follow the teachings of the **Buddha** (the Enlightened One). The Buddha is said to have taught:

- □ that everyone suffers;
- □ that, by following the right path, each person can eventually overcome that suffering. They will then reach a state of peace and everlasting bliss called **nirvana**.

Buddhists commit themselves to **three refuges**:

- □ I go to the Buddha for refuge.
- □ I go to the Dharma for refuge.
- □ I go to the Sangha for refuge.

The last of these statements, known as 'the third refuge', is recited daily by all Buddhists.

The **Dharma** (or teaching) is the truth about the way things are. A summary of this teaching is contained in the ***Dharmapada***, which is one of the most popular Buddhist texts.

The **Sangha**, or Buddhist community, plays a very important part in the growth and development of an awareness of the truth. Belonging to this community means becoming part of the Buddhist family. This whole community is made up of monks, nuns, and laypeople. Through belonging to the community Buddhists learn to put aside anything that would separate them from others by purifying their hearts of greed, ignorance and hatred. It then becomes possible to share with others those conditions of loving kindness and compassion which lie at the very heart of Buddhism. Today about 300,000,000 people follow the way of the Buddha for the sake of their own happiness and that of all other beings.

Key question   **What beliefs and practices lie at the heart of Buddhism?**

Work to do

1. The photograph below shows Buddhist monks outside a temple in London. Describe the clothes that they are wearing. What is particularly distinctive about them?

2. Carry out some research of your own to discover some information about the Buddhist community in Britain. Is there a Buddhist temple close to you? If so, try to arrange a visit.

Key words   **Buddha:** 'the Enlightened One', usually applied to Siddhartha Gautama Buddha (the Buddha), founder of the Buddhist religion. According to tradition, he was one of a succession of buddhas, past and future

Dharma: the teaching and religious principles at the heart of Buddhism

Dharmapada: an important book in the Buddhist scriptures consisting of 423 verses of sayings of the Buddha arranged in 26 chapters

nirvana: indescribable state of bliss that those who have been enlightened have reached

Sangha: the whole Buddhist community

three refuges: (also called the three jewels); the basic commitments of the Buddhist

6.2 Buddha – the early years

Focusing questions

- When and where was the Buddha born?
- Why did Buddhism develop outside India?
- Why did Gautama's father try to shield his son from the unpleasant side of life?
- Why did Gautama become homeless?

Siddhartha Gautama, who later came to be called the Buddha, was the founder of the Buddhist religion. The son of a rajah (king), he was born about 560 BCE and died at the age of 80. He lived in north-eastern India at a time when that area was one of the world's greatest intellectual and spiritual centres.

Statues of the Buddha outside a temple in Thailand

A thousand years before Gautama was born, the Aryan tribes had first entered India from the north-west and they spread to influence the whole of the sub-continent. Most of the Hindu holy books had already been written. Buddhism came as a great challenge to the Hindu religion and was later expelled from India. As we shall see, Buddhism has flowered and developed outside rather than inside its country of origin.

The birth of Siddhartha Gautama

As happens with the founders of many religions, all kinds of legends have grown up around the birth of Gautama. One such legend is that Maya (his mother) dreamed that a white elephant entered her womb and, ten months later, she gave birth to a child in the grove of Lumbini on the day of the full moon in May. The earth trembled and supernatural beings were present at the birth. His mother died seven days later because, legend says, she who has borne the Buddha cannot serve any other purpose. He was given two names:

☐ Siddhartha, meaning 'he who has reached his goal';
☐ Gautama, after a famous teacher from whom he was descended.

The young prince was brought up by his aunt in the greatest luxury and splendour. His father made sure of this since at Gautama's naming ceremony a wise man had said that the boy would either become a ruler or a wandering holy man. To make sure he became a ruler Gautama's father tried to remove him from any outside influences.

Rahula – chain

The young prince married a girl called Gopa (or Yashodara). According to legend she was outstanding for her beauty, modesty and breeding, yet when she had a son her husband called him Rahula (chain). In the midst of all the luxury Siddhartha Gautama felt as if he was in chains. He decided to leave everything behind and become homeless.

Before leaving home, however, Siddhartha had three experiences which confronted him with the harsh realities of life outside his palace. On three consecutive days he saw the suffering of the world in three forms:

☐ as a frail old man – he saw how old age destroys memory, beauty and strength;
☐ as an invalid racked with pain – he was shocked to see pain and suffering and 'trembled like the reflection of the moon on rippling water';
☐ as mourners weeping with a funeral procession – he was concerned about the obvious distress caused by death.

In a fourth experience he met a wandering holy man, contented and joyful, travelling around with an alms bowl. He suddenly saw that all of life's pleasures and treasures were worthless. What he now longed for was true knowledge. He left his palace and family in the middle of the night and stole away to look for that knowledge.

Key question **What did Gautama learn from the three experiences which changed his whole life?**

In this extract the Buddha speaks about his own childhood:

I was spoiled, very spoiled. I anointed myself with only Benares sandalwood and dressed only in Benares cloth. Day and night a white sunshade was held over me. I had a palace for the winter, one for the summer and one for the rainy season. In the four months of the rainy season I did not leave the palace at all, and I was surrounded by female musicians.

☐ Why did the father of Gautama surround his son with so much luxury?

> ### Work to do
> **(a) What was unusual about the birth of Siddhartha Gautama?**
> **(b) Why do you think that myths and legends are often attached to the births of famous religious leaders? What do they tell us about the meaning and importance of the person?**
> **(c) Can you think of *one* similar legend attached to the birth of the founder of another religion?**

6.3 Buddha – the Enlightened One

- Which ways of reaching the truth did Siddhartha Gautama reject?
- How did Gautama understand the truth?
- On which four 'truths' did Buddha base the whole of his teaching?

After Siddhartha Gautama left home he began searching for knowledge, as many Indian holy men did at the time. He tried constant yoga exercises but they did not yield the knowledge that he was seeking. For six years he lived in extreme poverty and self-denial with five companions, but still he was dissatisfied. In desperation he left his friends and sat beneath a bodhi tree to meditate.

The enlightenment

Gautama sat beneath the tree going into deeper and deeper meditation. During the next three nights he went through three stages of enlightenment and resisted the temptations of **Mara**, the Evil One, who tried to persuade Gautama to enter nirvana at once. By the end of it he saw the whole truth of existence.

- ☐ On the first night of meditation he saw his previous lives pass before him.
- ☐ On the second night he saw with supernatural insight the cycle of birth, death and rebirth and recognised the law that governs it.
- ☐ On the third night he came to understand the Four Holy Truths – the knowledge of suffering, the source of suffering, the removal of suffering and the way to removing the suffering. These were to become the basis of his teaching.

After Gautama's enlightenment, when he became the Buddha (the Enlightened One), he was asked by the high God Brahma three times to help others towards enlightenment by teaching them. This the Buddha did.

He preached his first sermon at Benares and his five former companions became his first followers. Soon the number grew. People were convinced by the serene calm of the preacher. Buddha sent them out to spread the new teaching. Buddha himself travelled around India for 44 years living as a beggar-monk. At the age of 80, though, he was taken ill during a meal and died in the town of Kushinagara. Many legends surround his death: they describe his joyful entry into the final nirvana and the terrible earthquake that shook the land to show the significance of his cremation.

Key question What was the path to truth for Siddhartha Gautama and what was that truth?

This is how the Buddhist scriptures describe the three stages to the Buddha's enlightenment.

The first watch

In the first watch of the night Siddhartha found that he knew about his previous lives. He said: 'There I was so and so; that was my name; dead there, I came here.' In this way he remembered the thousands of births as though he were living them over and over again. When he had seen all his own births and deaths he thought of other living things and thought to himself:

'Again and again they must leave people they think of as their own, and must go on elsewhere, and that without ever stopping. Surely this world is unprotected and helpless, and like a wheel it goes round and round.

The second watch

During the second watch he saw that the death and rebirth of all living things depended on whether they had thought and done good or bad things during their lifetimes. He saw that the threat of death is always present and that creatures could never find a resting-place.

The third watch

Then as the third watch drew on he thought: 'Alas, all living things wear themselves out. Over and over again they are born, they age and die, pass on to a new life, and are reborn. What is more, greed and false hopes blind them and they are blind from birth. Frightened, they do not yet know how to get out of this great ill!' Siddhartha found that lack of self-knowledge was the key. Once you understand what caused all the problems that happened to living creatures, including yourself, and through that knew how to live your life, then birth, death and illness all would cease.

By now Siddhartha had achieved a correct and complete knowledge and he stood out in the world as a Buddha.

☐ Why do you think that a wheel is the chosen symbol of Buddhism?
☐ What does the rebirth of all creatures depend on?
☐ What is the 'great ill' mentioned in the third extract and how can people get out of it?

Work to do

1. **The photograph below shows the enlightenment of Buddha.**
   (a) What symbols can you see which illustrate the state of enlightenment into which the Buddha has passed?
   (b) What do you think the scenes to the left and to the right of Buddha symbolise?

Key words **Mara:** the Evil One, he tried to tempt the Buddha from his quest for enlightenment

The Buddhapadipa temple in Wimbledon, London

6.4 King Asoka

Focusing questions

- What experience in the early rule of King Asoka turned him towards non-violence?
- How did King Asoka try to put his belief in non-violence into practice?
- Why do Buddhists look upon this king as a particularly enlightened person?

Asoka was the grandson of the great Emperor Chandragupta, who threw off Greek rule in India after the death of Alexander the Great in 323 BCE. It is thought that Chandragupta was attracted by the teachings of a Hindu sect called the Jains which emphasised non-violence. Perhaps his views influenced his grandson, Asoka. Certainly Asoka did much to turn Buddhism into a religion, giving it in the process a strong non-violent emphasis.

Asoka the warrior

In his early days Asoka loved hunting and was a notable warrior. It is thought that he made war in 261 BCE on the kingdom of Kalinga on the eastern coast of India, took 150,000 captives and slew more than 100,000 of them. Whilst Asoka recognised his own responsibility for the slaughter, it so sickened him that he decided to adopt a non-violent way of life. He said that in future he would seek to win the hearts and minds of his people by the law of duty or holiness. By saying this Asoka was demonstrating that he was a convert to the teachings of the Buddha.

Asoka pillar in Vaisali, India

The edicts of Asoka

Asoka is best known for the many inscriptions or edicts which he had engraved and set up throughout his kingdom. Some of them can still be seen to this day. On one of them Asoka deliberately echoed the words of the Buddha, whilst on another he promised that he would extend peace and friendship to the followers of any religion in his kingdom.

Asoka did not actually proclaim Buddhism to be the offcial faith in his kingdom since he promised complete tolerance to members of other faiths. Yet Buddhism was certainly given a favourable status. Not only did it enjoy the king's protection at home but also his support in missions abroad.

Asoka the first Buddhist ruler

King Asoka was not without his critics in his lifetime. There were those who complained that he tried to interfere too much in the everyday lives of his subjects. Others felt that he carried things too far when he banned the slaughter of animals – even for food. After his death, Sri Lanka, where Asoka had earlier sent his son and daughter as missionaries, became the centre of Buddhist activity.

Yet Buddhist legends do hold King Asoka up as the supreme example of a holy Buddhist layman, a ruler who was only interested in the welfare of his subjects and someone who was well on his way to enlightenment. He was the first Buddhist ruler and was responsible for sending Buddhist missionaries to many different countries. He is also credited with building as many as 84,000 **stupas** (burial mounds) all over India.

Key question **What was the importance of King Asoka in the history of Buddhism and why is he treated with such respect by Buddhists?**

The words of King Asoka:

All people are my children. I desire that all animate beings should have security, self-control, peace of mind and joyousness.

I honour members of all sects . . . by doing this one strengthens one's own sect and helps the others, whilst by doing otherwise one harms one's own sect and does a disservice to others . . . Concord is best, with each hearing and respecting the other's teachings.

☐ Does this, the first edict, only extend to the human members of his kingdom or does it go beyond that? How do you know?

☐ Do you know what a 'sect' is? If not, try to find out.

☐ What did Asoka believe would happen to his own sect if he did not extend friendship to members of other sects?

> *Work to do*
>
> **In this chapter we have learnt that King Asoka was converted to a non-violent approach to life. Carry out some research of your own to find out the answers to these questions:**
>
> **(a) What is another name for non-violence?**
>
> **(b) What is the name of a Hindu lawyer who was converted to non-violence and used it as a weapon to remove the British from India?**
>
> **(c) Which Christian denomination is firmly established on the principle of non-violence?**

Key words **stupa:** originally a burial mound built over the ashes of a famous person. After the Buddha died, for instance, his remains were divided into eight parts and a stupa built over each of them

6.5 The two main schools of Buddhism

- What are the two main schools of Buddhism?
- What are the basic teachings of Theravada Buddhism?
- What are the basic teachings of Mahayana Buddhism?

In the centuries following the death of Gautama Buddha, Buddhism split into several sects (or schools). There are two main schools of Buddhism.

Theravada Buddhism

Theravada Buddhism (Theravada means 'the way of the elders') is the form that Buddhism takes in Sri Lanka, Burma, Thailand and other parts of South-East Asia. Its teachings are based on scriptures called the **Pali Canon**, which Theravadas believe to be the most accurate record of what the Buddha actually taught. The most important teachings of the scriptures, according to the Theravadas, are that Buddha was only a man, one of a succession of buddhas, and that enlightenment can be reached through following his example and teachings. In the Theravada Buddhist community there are two main groups of people:

- ☐ The first consists of monks and nuns, who are totally dependent on other Buddhists for their food and clothing. These people are totally free from all domestic duties and so, Theravada Buddhists think, have the best chance of reaching nirvana. The closest of all to enlightenment are the 'forest monks', who practise very strict meditation.
- ☐ The second is made up of householders, who achieve merit for a better future rebirth by making offerings of food, clothes and money to the monks. It is less likely that a layperson will reach nirvana and so anyone who is really serious about striving to reach enlightenment becomes a 'bhikkhu' (see 9.6) or monk.

Mahayana Buddhism

Mahayana Buddhists (Mahayana means 'the great vehicle') view Siddhartha Gautama Buddha as a superhuman figure. They also believe that there exist, have existed and will exist in the future many other buddhas, throughout the universe. There are also a number of heavenly buddhas, such as Amida (see 6.6).

The approach of Mahayana Buddhism claims to offer more possibilities for enlightenment than Theravada Buddhism. These opportunities are based on three principles which, it is held, are in keeping with the teachings of Gautama Buddha.

- ☐ People do not have to rely on their own efforts or become monks or nuns to reach nirvana. Instead they are helped towards enlightenment by **bodhisattvas**. Bodhisattvas make a vow that they will take other beings to enlightenment with them.
- ☐ Bodhisattvas and Mahayana Buddhist teachers use many means to help people reach nirvana, including mantras, **koans** (word puzzles), cutting wood or drawing water. Anything can act as a vehicle for enlightenment, anything can be your teacher.
- ☐ The Sangha is the community of *all* who practise the Buddha's teachings.

Mahanaya Buddhism is the most widespread of the Buddhist schools. It is sub-divided into many other schools and is the main form of Buddhism in Japan, Korea, Mongolia, China, Tibet and Nepal.

Key question **How do followers hope to reach enlightenment through Theravada and Mahayana Buddhism?**

Work to do

1. Here are some terms used in this section. Using the information that you have been given *and* by carrying out some research of your own, write about 100 words on each:

> **(a) Theravada Buddhism; (b) Mahayana Buddhism; (c) bodhisattvas; (d) koans**

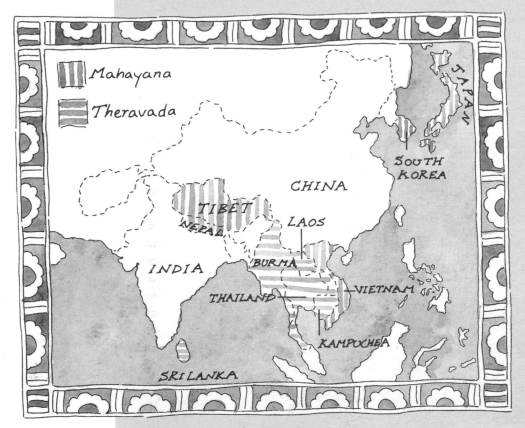

The areas where Mahayana and Theravada Buddhism are found

2. On this map you can see the main areas of the world where Mahayana and Theravada Buddhism are prevalent. Name *two* countries of the world where each of them is dominant.

Key words **bodhisattva:** Buddhist who has achieved enlightenment and who takes a vow that he or she will take other beings to enlightenment with them
koans: originally the sayings of famous Zen (see 6.6) masters or teachers. They are word puzzles used to startle people into spiritual awareness
Mahayana: the largest of the schools of Buddhism. It regards the Buddha as a superhuman figure
Pali Canon: the Buddhist scriptures
Theravada: one of the main sects of Buddhism, it claims to follow the way of the elders

6.6 The spread of Buddhism

Focusing questions

■ Which religion expanded in north India and brought about the decline of Buddhism there?
■ Why is Sri Lanka particularly important in the history of Buddhism?
■ In which two countries has Buddhism had to exist alongside Communist governments in recent years?

Buddhism, as we have seen, began in northern India but soon spread further afield. Even during the lifetime of the Buddha the new faith, under the drive of its founder, became very popular. Many were attracted to its message of release from life's ills – especially groups like the lower castes in Hindu society, who were despised by others.

Although the flame of Buddhism burned brightly in India for a thousand years after the death of the Buddha, it never achieved the status of an official religion in that country. When the Muslim religion began to expand in north India Buddhism went into decline in that region. Its popularity increased, however, in countries outside India.

The Shwe Dagon pagoda in Rangoon, Burma

Sri Lanka and Burma

Buddhism firmly established itself in the countries of Sri Lanka and Burma. It was during the 3rd century BCE that King Asoka sent his son, Mahinda, to Sri Lanka as a missionary. Once Buddhism was established there the Pali Canon was written down and for this reason the island of Sri Lanka has always enjoyed a special importance in the eyes of Buddhists. Even today some of the most important traditions and customs of Buddhism are celebrated there – especially in and around the cities of Kandy and Anuradhapura.

Asoka is also credited with having sent the first missionaries to Burma, where Theravada Buddhism took root and became the official religion of the country. Many beautiful temples were built and these have become places of pilgrimage – especially the Shwe Dagon pagoda in Rangoon.

China and Japan

When the Buddha's message was carried to China in the 1st century CE, that country was amongst the most important in the world. In the following century Emperor Han was converted to the faith and the principles of Buddhism were used to provide a blueprint for the organisation of Chinese society. A type of Buddhism focused on the **Amida** Buddha developed and many statues of Amida are still to be found in Buddhist temples. However, in recent years, following the Communist takeover of China in 1949, many Buddhist temples and shrines have either fallen into disrepair or have been destroyed.

Until 1860 Buddhism was the official religion of Japan but it was then replaced by Shintoism. Even so the religion continues to flourish in the country, especially in the form of **Zen Buddhism**.

Tibet

For centuries Tibet, which has its own distinct form of the religion, has had one of the strongest of all Buddhist traditions. In the past the political and religious leaders in the country have been under the leadership of the **Dalai Lama**. Under threat from Chinese Communists, however, he was forced to leave Tibet in 1959 and since then many monasteries and places of worship have been forcibly closed.

Buddhism elsewhere

Buddhism has established itself in almost all Western countries although there has never been a major influx of Buddhist immigrants. The vast majority of followers in Britain and the USA, for example, are Westerners who have turned to the faith. In particular, the practice of meditation has proved attractive to many people overwhelmed by the pressures of modern Western life.

Key question **Which countries has Buddhism spread to and what problems has it sometimes had to face?**

Work to do
The beautiful Shwe Dagon pagoda in Rangoon, Burma, is famous for three relics of the Buddha that it contains.
(a) Can you find out what a relic is and why relics play a very important role in many religions?
(b) Can you discover which particular relics of the Buddha are found in the Shwe Dagon pagoda?

Key words **Amida:** Buddha of 'Immeasurable Light', one of the five buddhas of Mahayana Buddhism. He is the ruler of the West, the Pure Land to which the setting sun carries the souls of the dying
Dalai Lama: spiritual head of Tibetan Buddhism
Zen Buddhism: form of Mahayana Buddhism which grew up and has had the greatest impact in China and Japan, it puts its greatest emphasis on meditation

7. THE SACRED WRITINGS OF BUDDHISM

7.1 The Buddhist scriptures

Focusing questions

- What is the Pali Canon?
- What do Theravada Buddhists believe happened to the material in the Pali Canon before it was written down?
- What additional material do Mahayana Buddhists accept as being sacred?

The Buddha was a very skilful teacher. He made use of many methods to put over his message – parables, illustrations from nature, similes, metaphors, questions and answers, discussions and debates. Yet he did not write anything down himself or leave behind a written record of his teaching. When he died his disciples began to gather his teachings together. The scriptures of the Theravada school are the best known, but the Mahayana schools also have their own scriptures. These have almost all now been translated into Western languages.

The scriptures of the Theravada Buddhists

The Theravada Buddhists believe that shortly after the death of the Buddha there was a council at Rajagaha. At that council senior monks listened to and checked a list of the rules which applied to the life of the Sangha and also a collection of the teachings of the Buddha. These two collections were then passed down by word of mouth from monk to monk for hundreds of years. Finally, in the 1st century BCE they, and a third section which had now been added, were written down in the Pali language. These scriptures are known as the Pali Canon, and its three sections are called the **Tipitaka**. They are still read and recited in their original language wherever possible, although the use of translations is perfectly acceptable among people who do not know Pali. Theravada Buddhists believe that the Pali Canon (see 7.2) is an accurate record of the teaching of Gautama Buddha. The other important Theravada scripture is the *Questions of King Milinda*, which records a dialogue which took place in the 2nd century CE between the monk Nagasena and the Greek king Menander ('Milinda' in Pali).

The scriptures of the Mahayana Buddhists

Mahayana Buddhists have their own version of much of what is found in the Pali Canon but they have also added other works. They claim that these additional works are authoritative as the 'Buddha word'. Although it is not easy to date them accurately, they seem to have first seen the light of day sometime between the 2nd century BCE and the 2nd century CE. One of the most famous of these additional works, or 'sutras' as they are called, is the *Vimalakirti Sutra*, which is about a householder, Vimalakirti, who is more holy than all the bodhisattvas.

The hidden scriptures of the Tibetan Buddhists

Tibetan Buddhists believe that many scriptures were hidden until the community was ready to receive, and understand, their teachings. These hidden scriptures are still being found today, the most widely used being the *Tibetan Book of the Dead*.

Key question   In what different ways have the teachings of Buddha been handed down?

Work to do

Here are some questions about the Buddhist holy books. You will need to carry out some research of your own before you can answer most of them. You can find some information in 7.2.

(a) What are the main books of Theravada and Mahayana Buddhism called?

(b) In what language are the books of Theravada and Mahayana Buddhism written?

(c) Why is the term 'basket' used for the most important Buddhist holy books?

(d) What is the second basket about and why are the contents of this book very important for Buddhists?

(e) What is the link between a lotus flower and the Buddhist scriptures?

Key words   **Tipitaka:** literally 'the three baskets' – the three sections into which the Pali Canon is divided

7.2 Tipitaka

Focusing questions

■ Where does the term Tipitaka come from and what does it refer to?
■ What does the *Vinaya Pitaka* contain?
■ What does the *Sutta Pitaka* contain?
■ What does the *Abhidharma Pitaka* contain?

The three sections of the Pali Canon are known as the Tipitaka – or 'three baskets'. If you can imagine builders working together and passing baskets of material from one to another you can probably work out why they are called the three baskets. The material was handed down from one generation to the next by word of mouth. Eventually, in the 1st century BCE monks wrote the scriptures down on long strips of palm leaf and arranged them as three separate collections.

The *Vinaya Pitaka*

This book contains the rules of discipline for the monastic Sangha. The version of the *Vinaya Pitaka* written in Pali has five volumes, although Mahayana Buddhists add one more. In the Pali version there are 227 rules for men and additional rules for women. They start with the most serious faults – such as sexual misconduct or murder – for which the punishment is being thrown out of the order. A list of less serious offences – such as falsely accusing another monk of misconduct – prescribes a period of probation for the offender. Finally the least serious offences are to be forgiven after an admission of guilt.

In addition the *Vinaya Pitaka* also stipulates that a monk is allowed just eight possessions – an alms bowl, a needle, a razor, a toothpick, a belt and three robes. In certain climates shoes are considered to be a luxury, whilst in other places they are treated as a necessity.

The *Sutta Pitaka*

The word 'sutta' means 'thread' and this collection contains the threads of the teachings of the Buddha. The *Sutta Pitaka* contains the *Dharmapada* with its account of the Four Noble Truths and the Eightfold Path (see 8.2 and 8.3). Written in both verse and prose, the *Dharmapada* is so highly valued by Buddhists that many of them learn it off by heart so that they can regularly recite it.

The *Abhidharma Pitaka* or 'higher teachings'

The development of the *Abhidharma Pitaka* began during the lifetime of the Buddha when he indicated that there was a layer of explanation over and above (abhi) his teachings (Dharma).

Key question How did the Tipitaka come together and what is it made up of?

This analysis of 'right speech' – one of the ingredients in the Eightfold Path – is taken from the *Abhidharma Pitaka*.

> *What is right speech?*
> 1 *Abstaining from false speech.*
> 2 *Abstaining from slanderous speech.*
> 3 *Abstaining from harsh speech.*
> 4 *Abstaining from frivolous speech.*

What is 'abstaining'?
'. . . avoiding, desisting from, not committing, not doing, being
guiltless of, not overstepping the limit of, destroying the
causeway to . . .'

☐ Explain, with examples, how you understand false, slanderous, harsh and
frivolous speech.

☐ Does 'abstaining from' simply mean not doing something or is it more
than that?

Work to do
**Answer each of these questions about the Tipitaka using the information in
this unit.**

    (a) Where does the name Tipitaka come from?

    (b) How many rules are there in the *Vinaya Pitaka*?

    **(c) What are the eight possessions that a Buddhist monk is allowed to
have?**

    (d) In which collection is the *Dharmapada* found?

    (e) Why is the *Dharmapada* particularly important?

    (f) What is to be found in the *Abhidharma Pitaka*?

    (g) Why is the *Abhidharma Pitaka* so called?

Studying the Tipitaka

8. THE BELIEFS AND IDEAS OF BUDDHISM

8.1 The Three Universal Truths

Focusing questions
■ What is anicca?
■ What is anatta?
■ What happens when a person reaches nirvana?

According to Buddhist teaching there are Three Universal Truths which are the foundation of all human existence.

Anicca

Anicca is the constant change and lack of permanence which characterises everything in the world. Experience teaches us that in human existence all things come and go without anything, not even human existence itself, being permanent. For many people this may be very disturbing but it is, in fact, very important as it means that a person's personality is always growing and changing. It is this growing personality which is a person's 'true self'.

To express this impermanence Buddhists often speak of life as a series of

Handing the Olympic flame from one person to another is a possible analogy to explain the idea of anicca

candles, each one (apart from the first) being lit by the one that has gone before. In this way the same light can be said to have proceeded along the line, with each candle only having a brief, temporary existence. Other analogies are also used in Buddhist literature to explain this difficult idea.

Anatta

The idea of **anatta** follows on from anicca. There is no unchangeable, permanent self or soul in anything or anybody. Yet there is a 'person' and the person is made up of five components or **skandhas**. They are:

☐ the physical body (rupa);
☐ feelings or sensations (vedana);
☐ an awareness of things outside us (sanna);
☐ our thoughts, ideas, wishes, dreams (sankhara);
☐ our consciousness, which binds all of these different components together and so forms a person (vinnana).

Yet, as we have said, these five components do not make up a permanent, unchangeable self. If they appear to us to do so it is only an illusion. When a person dies all of the skandhas fall apart and are reassembled in another body, according to a different pattern. It is only when nirvana is reached that the skandhas are finally dispersed since there is no further need for them. When this happens the process of becoming has been completed and a state of pure joy is reached (see 8.5).

Dukkha

In this life everything changes. However wonderful life might be now, change must inevitably lead to suffering. This belief (**Dukkha**) is one of the Four Noble Truths and we will find out more about it in 8.2.

Key question **What are the three characteristics of human existence according to Buddhist teaching?**

> ### Work to do
> Someone once asked the Buddha whether existence was an illusion. He kept quiet and offered no answer. When a disciple asked him afterwards why he had said nothing the Buddha replied:
>
> > If I had answered that anything is eternal it would have been misunderstood.
> > If I had said that nothing exists that, too, would have been misunderstood.
>
> After reading his answer can you begin to explain why the Buddha offered no answer to the original question?

Key words **anatta:** Buddhist belief that there is no permanent, unchanging self or soul in any person or any thing
anicca: Buddhist belief that there is a constant change and lack of permanence in the world
dukkha: Buddhist belief that pain or suffering comes inevitably as the result of change
skandhas: five components that make up human nature

8.2 The Four Noble Truths

Focusing questions

- What four sights did Siddhartha Gautama see outside the royal palace and what did they teach him?
- What lies at the heart of all suffering?
- What is the Middle Way and which two extremes does it lie between?

The Four Noble Truths are the insights (see 6.2) that the Buddha received as he sat under the bodhi tree.

All life is suffering

It was only when Siddhartha Gautama saw an old man, a sick man, a dead man and a holy man outside his palace that he began to understand the true nature of suffering. He realised that nothing lasts for ever and even the happiest moments in life disappear like vapour into the air.

The cause of suffering is desire

Suffering is caused by desire (**tanha**) for people, things and continued existence. It is this desire that breeds ignorance and self-delusion and these keep us bound to this world and the round of continual rebirth.

Even if a desire is temporarily satisfied, the natural world is bound to laws which bring about continual change, so that lasting satisfaction is never achieved. If we remain in the grip of desire then our suffering can only increase. Instead we must find the remedy and so be released from the vice-like grip that desire can exert on us.

There can be a release from suffering

This is the Buddha's remedy for the ills of this world. A person must begin by eliminating all selfish desires and the craving for attachment to this world. To do this successfully a person must avoid either of two extremes – giving in to their selfish desires or walking the path of self-denial.

All people must follow the Middle Way

The Buddha provided several pictures to help his followers understand this path. He spoke of the **Middle Way** as being like:

- ☐ a tank of water for those who are thirsty;
- ☐ a fire to warm up those who are suffering from the cold;
- ☐ a garment to cover those who are naked;
- ☐ a caravan leader for the merchants;
- ☐ a mother for her children;
- ☐ a boat for those who need a ferry;
- ☐ a lamp for those who are surrounded by darkness.

You will find this Middle Way (the Eightfold Path) explained in section 8.3.

Key question What are the Four Noble Truths on which the teaching of the Buddha is based?

The Buddha explains just what suffering is:

> *This, O Bhikkhus, is the Noble Truth of Suffering; death is suffering; presence of objects we hate is suffering; separation from objects we love is suffering; not to obtain what we desire is suffering.*
> *Briefly, the fivefold clinging to existence is suffering.*
> *All existence is dukkha (suffering).*

☐ Think of *three* examples of suffering in today's world which help you to understand the Buddha's explanation of what suffering is.

Work to do

In this extract the Buddha explains to his followers the importance of following the Middle Way:

> There are two extremes, O monks, that should not be practised.
>   And what are these two?
>   That devoted to passions and luxury – which is low, unworthy, vulgar and useless; and that devoted to self-mortification, which is painful, unworthy and useless.
>   By avoiding these two extremes, the Perfect One (the Buddha) has gained the enlightenment.

(a) What two extremes are monks to avoid in their search for enlightenment?

(b) What is the Middle Way and what can it alone lead to?

(c) Why do you think that Buddhism has been called 'the Balanced Way'? Do you think that this means sitting on the fence, not being committed to anything?

(d) How did the Buddha himself achieve enlightenment?

Key words **Middle Way:** path taught by the Buddha which leads to enlightenment and the end of all suffering

tanha: means 'thirst'; a strong desire for things that do not satisfy or are not necessary

8.3 The Eightfold Path

Focusing questions
■ What is brought under control by following the Eightfold Path?
■ Why are most Buddhists vegetarians?
■ What part does meditation play in following the path towards enlightenment?

The last of the Four Noble Truths is to seek release from desire and suffering by following the Middle Way or Eightfold Path. The different steps along this pathway are rather like the spokes in a wheel. Although they each have a separate identity of their own, they gain their real strength from their unity together. Yet to gain an understanding of the whole, one must understand the different parts that make up that whole.

The Eightfold Path provides a blueprint which enables the Buddhist to conquer the greed and hatred which are the root causes of suffering. Its different aspects encourage a person towards new ways of thinking, speaking and acting.

1. **Right understanding of the Four Noble Truths:** from this individuals go on to begin to understand themselves and the universe in which they live.

2. **Right thoughts:** loving thoughts to all living things, even the most humble.

3. **Right speech:** people's speech is very important since the words that come out of their mouths not only reveal their own true character but also have the power to hurt and harm others. Their speech, therefore, must always be pure, true and noble. Falsehood, slander and vile language must be strenuously avoided.

4. **Right action:** involves acting morally, being considerate to other people and showing kindness towards all living creatures. For the vast majority of Buddhists this rules out the killing of animals for food. They are vegetarians. Very strict Buddhists take great care that no living thing is killed, even accidentally. It also means abstaining from those things that lessen self-control such as alcohol.

5. **Right livelihood:** any occupation that involves violence, such as that of a soldier, is ruled out. As a Buddhist is forbidden to harm any living thing he is unlikely to work as a butcher or a fisherman. Nor is a Buddhist allowed to earn his living from following his religion. Because of this a Buddhist monk is not paid, but is totally dependent on the gifts of other believers.

6. **Right effort:** this is to banish all evil thoughts, including anything that would stop a person from following the Middle Way.

7. **Right mindfulness:** all those who are seeking to follow the Middle Way must be continually aware of the needs of others rather than themselves. As this is not the natural thing to do it requires considerable self-discipline.

8. **Right concentration:** the aim of being able to concentrate is to become calm, collected, at peace with oneself and with the world generally. This is why meditation plays such an important part in Buddhism. Through this Buddhists become highly skilled in controlling their thoughts, their feelings and their breathing. They allow nothing to distract them from their efforts to follow the Middle Way.

There are no rewards for following this path – apart from the sense of inner peace that it brings. Yet one of the Buddha's titles is 'Tathagatha' ('Gone thus') and in following the path each Buddhist is following the Master towards enlightenment.

Key question **What is the Eightfold Path and why is it a very important aspect of Buddhist belief and practice?**

Work to do

1. **(a) What do you think is the purpose and the importance of each part of the Eightfold Path?**
   (b) What problems might face a Buddhist who is trying to follow the Eightfold Path today?
   (c) Can you think of any aspects of personal behaviour which are not covered by the Eightfold Path? If so, what are they, and what do you think the Buddha might have said about them? (Remember that the path is intended to deal with the causes of suffering.)

2. **This photograph shows a group of Buddhists meditating. Find out as much as you can about this religious practice. Try to discover in particular:**
   (a) how the practice of meditation is linked to the teachings in the Eightfold Path;
   (b) which form of meditation is practised in particular by Japanese Buddhist monks;
   (c) what meditation exercises a Buddhist is likely to perform and what he or she hopes to achieve through them;
   (d) why many people in this country who are not Buddhists use meditation to help them cope with the stresses and strains of modern life.

Novice monks meditating, Thailand

8.4 The Ten Precepts

Focusing questions
- What are the Ten Precepts and who must keep them?
- What is ahimsa?
- What is celibacy?

The **Precepts** are the promises, or vows, that Buddhists make. Monks follow ten precepts; lay Buddhists keep the first five. The following four they keep when they are on meditation retreats and during certain religious festivals. These precepts are based upon fundamental Buddhist beliefs about life and the universe.

1. **To refrain from harming any living thing:** no living thing may be intentionally harmed – this belief is called ahimsa (see 3.5). An action is wrong if the intention behind it is wrong. Non-harming starts in the heart and so all Buddhists are encouraged to cultivate 'loving kindness'.

2. **To refrain from taking what is not given:** all lay Buddhists must conduct their personal and business lives in a blameless way. A failure to live and conduct one's life in this way means that other people are defrauded whilst the perpetrator loses his or her chances of enjoying happiness. A monk must not beg or take what does not belong to him but must be totally dependent on the generosity of others. To do otherwise is stealing.

3. **To refrain from a misuse of the senses:** the ideal for all Buddhists is to live chastely, within their chosen life-style, and not abuse their sexuality. Adultery, unchastity and promiscuity are always wrong. However, only monks are expected to follow a life of **celibacy**.

4. **To refrain from wrong speech:** anyone who lies or withholds the truth blurs the distinction between truth and falsehood. To do so destroys any hope that a person might have of achieving personal happiness.

5. **To refrain from taking intoxicants that cloud the mind:** if the mind is blurred the person cannot lead the kind of thoughtful life that is essential for happiness.

6. **To refrain from taking food other than at the times prescribed by monastic routine**

7. **To refrain from dancing, singing, music and other unseemly activities**

8. **To refrain from the use of garlands, perfumes and unguents (deodorants) and from things that tend to beautify the person**

9. **To refrain from using high and luxurious beds**

10. **To refrain from accepting gold and silver**

Key question What are the Ten Precepts?

Work to do
Buddhists believe that nothing in the world is permanent, since everything is in the process of changing. This is true of the teachings (Dharma) of the Buddha as of everything else. To illustrate this the Buddha told a parable:

Monks I will teach you Dharma – the parable of the raft – for getting across, not for retaining. Listen to it, pay careful attention, and I will speak. It is like a man, monks, who as he is going on a journey should see a great stretch of water, this bank with dangers and fears, the farther bank secure and without fears, but there may be neither a boat for crossing over, nor a bridge across for going from the not-beyond to the beyond. It occurs to him that in order to cross over from the perils of this bank to the security of the other bank, he should fashion a raft out of grass and sticks, branches and foliage so that he could cross over to the beyond in safety. When he has done this and has crossed over to the beyond, it occurs to him that the raft has been very useful and he wonders if he ought to proceed taking it with him packed on his head or shoulders. What do you think, monks?

(a) What is a parable?

(b) What is Dharma?

(c) What do you think that the Buddha wanted to convey by the journey that this man took and the great stretch of water that he came across?

(d) What does the safe bank in the distance stand for?

(e) What does the raft in the parable signify, and what is the significance of the fact that it is made out of ordinary things that need to be bound together before they have any strength?

(f) What do you think that the Buddha meant by saying that the raft, and the parable, are 'for getting across, not for retaining'?

Key words **celibacy:** acceptance of the unmarried state, involving abstention from all sexual relations

Precepts: commitments lay Buddhists and monks live by

8.5 Rebirth and nirvana

Focusing questions
- What do Buddhists mean by the 'samsara circle'?
- What is karma and why is it such an important Buddhist belief?
- What is reincarnation?
- What is distinctive about the Buddhist belief in nirvana?

The origins of Buddhism lie in Hinduism, so early Buddhist thought owes much to the older religion. This quotation comes from the Upanishads (see 1.2), a Hindu holy book.

In this sort of cycle of existence (samsara) what is the good of enjoyment of desires, when after a man has fed upon them there is seen repeatedly his return here to earth?

From the quotation we are introduced to two basic Buddhist ideas – those of samsara and karma. Through them we are also introduced to another very important Buddhist belief – that of nirvana (see 6.1).

Samsara and karma

Samsara means literally 'continuation' or 'carrying on' and to the Buddhist it conveys the idea that a person has more than one life – when they die they are born again, or reincarnated. Life to the Buddhist is an almost endless round of existences – a person is born, lives, dies and is born again and again. This process is known as the 'samsara circle'.

The force which keeps the wheel of samsara turning is called karma. It is karma that causes rebirths. The word itself means 'deed' or 'act' and conveys the important notion that what a person does creates a kind of force which is carried over from one life to the next. If a person, therefore, leads a bad life in their present existence their next life will be one of a lower status. A good life, on the other hand, will ensure that a person returns at a higher level in the next existence. The only way to escape the law of karma is to stop being reborn and that only happens when a person reaches enlightenment, or nirvana.

Nirvana

If we try to describe nirvana we come immediately to a problem. Nirvana is a state of existence to be enjoyed and not described. Yet we can find a clue or two to what nirvana is by looking at the word itself. It simply means 'going out' as when a candle expires because there is no more wax to burn. Nirvana is that higher state of consciousness in which all greed, hatred and ignorance are exhausted, so releasing a person from the cycle of samsara.

When nirvana is reached an individual has finally attained his or her goal. What happens beyond that the Buddha himself and his followers are not prepared to say. This is because the process for reaching nirvana is almost infinitely long, although it is held out as a real objective for every Buddhist. You can find out what the Buddha had to say about nirvana by reading the extract in this section.

Key question What do Buddhists mean by the 'cycle of existence' and how can that cycle eventually be broken?

The Buddha is recorded as saying:

> *There is, disciples, a condition where there is neither earth nor water, nor fire nor air, nor the sphere of infinite consciousness, nor the sphere of the void, nor the sphere of neither perception nor non-perception . . . that condition, disciples, do I neither call a coming nor a going, nor a standing still nor a falling away . . . but that condition is without fixity . . . it is the end of woe.*

☐ What is not true about nirvana?
☐ What is true about nirvana?

Work to do

Buddhists believe in a linked chain of lives which they call 'rebirth' whilst Sikhs and Hindus believe in the reincarnation of the soul.

(a) What is reincarnation?

(b) Find out the main arguments that Buddhists, Sikhs and Hindus put forward to support these beliefs.

(c) What belief do Christians, Muslims and Jews hold about life after death and how does it contrast with belief in reincarnation?

(d) Are there any aspects of human life and experience which might lead you to believe in rebirth or reincarnation?

Painted images of the seated Buddha, Tibet

9. BUDDHIST WORSHIP

9.1 Symbols and images

Focusing questions
- What do the three images of the Buddha symbolise?
- What is a mandala?
- What does the Wheel of Life symbolise?

It is never easy to put abstract religious ideas and beliefs into words. Buddhists believe that their deepest feelings can best be expressed in pictures rather than words. For this reason Buddhism is rich in symbols and images. There are three important symbols which are used by Buddhist worshippers.

Images of the Buddha
Images of the Buddha fall into three main categories.

The Buddha seated: one of the commonest positions shows the Buddha in the lotus position. This is a posture of meditation with the back straight, hands folded palms upward across the lap and with each foot resting on the opposite thigh. This is thought to resemble the lotus flower with a long stem rising above the water. Many Buddhists see this image as a symbol of spiritual growth which raises one above the suffering of the world.

The Buddha standing: these statues usually show the Buddha giving a blessing, with one hand raised in front of his breast.

The Buddha lying down: this symbolises the Buddha entering nirvana at the end of his life. Sometimes the soles of his feet are shown covered with symbols like the wheel and lotus to indicate that he was a very special man.

Mandalas (or 'circles')
These are sacred diagrams which are used widely by Buddhists, especially in Tibet. They may be painted on 'tankas' (or scrolls), but are usually three-dimensional in form, sometimes being made from coloured sand. As with similar designs in Hinduism, Buddhist mandalas are symmetrical patterns of triangles, circles and squares. Sometimes they contain images of the Buddha and often images of future buddhas called bodhisattvas (see 6.5). Mandalas are used as aids to concentration, helping the soul towards union with the Divine.

The Wheel of Life
The Wheel of Life is the name given to a particular kind of mandala illustrating the Buddhist's idea of life. The main part of the wheel is a large circle which is held in the grip of a fierce dragon called Yama, who symbolises change and death. At the centre of the circle are three animals:

- [ ] the cock, symbolising greed or desire;
- [ ] the snake, symbolising hatred;
- [ ] the pig, symbolising confusion and chaos.

These three 'evils' stand in the way of a person's enlightenment. In a narrow strip around this circle are many figures rising and falling, showing that people may go forward or back on the path to enlightenment.

What are the main symbols and images in Buddhism and why are they used?

Work to do

This drawing shows the Buddhist Wheel of Life. Answer the following questions about it:

(a) What is the name of the demon above the wheel and what does he symbolise?

(b) Which three animals are at the centre of the wheel and what do they symbolise? What can they prevent Buddhists from doing?

(c) Why are there drawings of figures rising and falling in the narrow circle around the outside?

(d) Why do you think that the Buddha is shown preaching in many parts of the wheel?

Key words **The Wheel of Life:** a type of painting which illustrates the Buddhist understanding of life in samsara

9.2 Worship at the vihara

Focusing questions

■ Why do most Buddhist temples have images of the buddhas or bodhisattvas in their shrine-rooms?
■ What happens when a Buddhist worshipper enters the shrine-room in a vihara?
■ What offerings are presented to the image of the Buddha?

All branches of Buddhism have forms of puja (worship) and this means showing respect for whatever is thought to be of ultimate value. In other religions this is God, but in Buddhism it is described by such phrases as 'emptiness' or the 'state of enlightenment'. This state of enlightenment has been clearly shown by the buddhas or bodhisattvas of the past and the images of these people are honoured by finding a place in the shrine-room of the temple or monastery (**vihara**). Such images are 'fingers' pointing a way to the ultimate reality.

Acts of worship

Acts of Buddhist worship take place each day both in the home and also in the vihara. As the body, language and thoughts are involved in every act of worship the visitor to a vihara will see silent meditation, teaching, the making of offerings and physical prostration, and hear chanting during the act of worship.

Before entering the shrine-room worshippers take off their shoes. In Eastern

Buddhist temple offerings, Thailand

countries this is a sign of respect, but in Western monasteries this practice is retained largely for the sake of tradition. The worshipper then places his or her hands together and makes a prostration before the image, either from a kneeling (Theravada) position or a standing (Tibetan) position. Either before or after this prostration an offering is made. There are three basic offerings that can be made:

☐ flowers – as these will wither and die they are a reminder of the impermanence of life;
☐ light – a light burns brightly and dispels darkness;
☐ incense – the smell of incense lasts and reminds the worshipper of the fragrance of the Buddha's teaching.

Mahayana Buddhists make a sevenfold offering to the Buddha and this is often symbolised by seven bowls of water, which can be used, for example, for drinking, bathing or washing the feet.

Finally, after the offerings have been made, the three refuges and the Five Precepts are recited. Some mantras are said, and there is a period of silent meditation. Usually some form of teaching is then given before the act of worship ends.

Key question **What are the main characteristics of an act of Buddhist worship in a vihara?**

This prayer often accompanies an offering in a Buddhist vihara:

I make the offering to the Buddha with these flowers
And through this merit may there be release
Even as these flowers must fade
So my body goes towards destruction.

☐ Why do you think that flowers are considered to be a suitable offering and what do they remind the worshipper about?

Work to do
Offerings of a lamp or of incense can be made as part of Buddhist worship. Below you will find two prayers that can be said as these offerings are made. Read them carefully before answering the questions which follow:

1. *With this lamp [candle] which shines brightly dispelling the darkness, I make my offering to the truly enlightened lamp of the three worlds, who dispels the darkness of ignorance.*
   (a) Why is a lamp thought to be a particularly appropriate offering to make?
   (b) Who do you think is 'the truly enlightened lamp of the three worlds'?
   (c) What does 'the truly enlightened lamp' do?

2. *To him of fragrant body and face,*
   Fragrant with infinite values,
   To the Buddha I make offering with fragrant incense.
   (a) What does the word 'fragrant' mean?
   (b) With what is the Buddha said to be fragrant?

Key words **vihara:** literally 'abode' or 'station', a temple or monastery

9.3 Prayer in Buddhism

Focusing questions

- What is a mala and what use might a Buddhist make of it whilst praying?
- What are prayer wheels and what use is made of them in Tibetan Buddhism?
- What is the 'Jewel in the Lotus'?

All Buddhists honour Siddhartha Gautama because he not only discovered the path to enlightenment for himself but he also shared that path with others. When they come into the shrine-room of the vihara and see a statue of the Buddha worshippers are inspired by the body and face of the image. From it they can see the loving kindness, compassion, joy and equanimity of the Buddha. These are qualities that all Buddhists aspire to. Through praying a Buddhist hopes to develop those qualities.

Turning prayer wheels at the Monkey Temple, Kathmandu, Nepal

Prayer in Tibetan Buddhism

Tibetan Buddhists have different religious practices from those of Buddhists in other countries. To help them pray, for example, they make use of a set of prayer beads (a **mala**) which can contain 108, 54 or 27 beads. Made of seeds, wood or plastic these beads have two main uses:

☐ They can be used to count the number of prostrations or prayers being said.
☐ They can be used to help concentrate the thoughts during meditation. With each bead a mantra is chanted or the name of a buddha or bodhisattva is recited. The circle of beads may contain three bigger beads to remind the worshipper of the three refuges – the Buddha, the Dharma and the Sangha.

Tibetan Buddhists also believe that when certain sounds or words (called mantras) are recited many times they arouse good vibrations within the person. Repeated often enough the mantra is able to open up the mind to a higher form of consciousness.

The greatest mantra – Om mani padme hum – is known as the 'Jewel in the Lotus' since it is thought to be at the heart of the Buddha's teaching. It is also inscribed on revolving bronze cylinders called **prayer wheels**. Every temple and monastery has a set of prayer wheels which people spin round so that the vibrations can be sent in all directions. Sometimes the prayer wheels are driven by water or electric power.

Prayer in other countries

In Sri Lanka and Thailand the viharas are always open and Buddhists try to spend some time each day worshipping. After presentation of offerings to the Buddha time is spent in prayer. They do not, however, use prayer beads or wheels as aids to prayer.

Key question   **What part does prayer play in Buddhist worship and what aids might Buddhists use to help them pray?**

Work to do

1. (a) What is the name used for a Buddhist's set of prayer beads?
   (b) Why do you think that the followers of several different religions make use of prayer beads?

2. The photograph opposite shows a row of prayer wheels.
   (a) In which country would you be likely to see these prayer wheels?
   (b) Why are prayer wheels an important element in Buddhist life and what do Buddhists believe happens when they are turned?

3. In a radio programme, *Worlds of Faith*, broadcast in 1983, a practising Buddhist had this to say about prayer:
   Prayer doesn't exist in Buddhism as such because there's no one to talk to. In my devotions I say to myself 'To the best of my ability, I shall try to emulate the life of the Buddha.' So I have my shrine-room, and even my children before they go to their work or to their colleges, they do their devotion, and only after their devotion, they set out.
   It's almost the same as having a portrait of your parents to remind you of the love that they had for you.
   (a) Why doesn't prayer exist, as such, in Buddhism?
   (b) What does the speaker promise to do when he says his devotions?
   (c) How does a portrait of their parents remind Buddhists of the importance of their devotions?

Key words   **mala:** set of prayer beads used by Hindus and Sikhs, as well as some Buddhists
prayer wheels: revolving bronze cylinders upon which sacred phrases are inscribed; used by monks (lamas) in Tibet

9.4 Uposatha days and rains retreat

Focusing questions

■ What are uposatha days?
■ What was the original purpose of an uposatha day?
■ What is a 'rains retreat' and why was it originally introduced?

There are many Buddhist celebrations. In this section we will look at just two of them. Although lay Buddhists are involved in these celebrations they mainly concern monks, and take place largely within the confines of a monastery.

Uposatha days

Originally all monks in a certain area came together once a fortnight – every full moon and every new moon – so that they could confess to one another any failures to keep the monastic code of discipline. Whilst this particular custom is no longer observed, these two days are times of intense religious activity for Buddhists, as, to a lesser extent, are the half-moon days which fall between them.

These **uposatha days** are also times set aside for lay Buddhists to visit their nearest monastery. On these days no agricultural work is done and people abstain from eating meat and fish. They take the opportunity to make offerings to the monks, especially of food, and pay respect to the nearest image of the Buddha.

In those countries where Theravada Buddhism is particularly powerful worshippers may well choose to spend most of the day in the monastery, where they will perform religious exercises, listen to a sermon, recite religious mantras

Lay Buddhists visiting their monastery in England

and take part in some form of meditation. Most important of all, they will adopt the ten precepts for the day, including abstaining from all food after noon, not wearing jewellery or other adornments and not sleeping in a grand bed. By doing this they are becoming monks for a short time.

Rains retreat

In the early days of Buddhism monks who wandered from place to place were compelled to settle in one place during the monsoon season since the heavy rain ruled out travelling. The custom still remains and in Theravada countries many lay Buddhists offer monks places to lodge for three months. This period is known as the 'rains retreat'.

At the end of the retreat monks gather together to seek forgiveness for any wrong act that they have committed. This gathering-together is private to the monks and commemorates the rains retreat in the seventh year after the Buddha's enlightenment, which he spent in one of the lower heavens where his mother had been reborn. On the last day of the retreat he came down to earth and was attended by the kings of the gods. (Buddhists believe that there are different states of existence into which it is possible to be reborn – see 10.3. One of these is the realm of the gods.)

Either on the last day of the retreat, or shortly afterwards, lay Buddhists present new robes to the monks. This new garment, the **kathina** robe, is presented to a representative of the monastery and is made traditionally by sewing patches together. The ceremony that accompanies the presentation is unusual in that it is the only ceremony involving lay people for which there is authority in the Buddhist scriptures.

Key question **What particular things do Buddhists do during uposatha days and rains retreat which they do not do during other acts of worship?**

Work to do
1. (a) How often are uposatha days held?
   (b) Which are the most important of the uposatha days?
   (c) What do many Buddhists abstain from on uposatha days?
   (d) What might a pious Buddhist do on an uposatha day?
   (e) Most religions have one day a week devoted, in the main, to worship. Why do you think that these special days of worship have become very important to religious people?

2. (a) What is the rains retreat and what event in the life of the Buddha is commemorated on the last day of the retreat?
   (b) When is the kathina ceremony held?
   (c) What is unusual about the kathina ceremony?
   (d) What is traditionally presented during the kathina ceremony and how is the gift made?

Key words **kathina:** robes presented to the monks by ordinary Buddhists after the end of the rains retreat

uposatha days: observance days, held on each full moon and new moon day, as well as on half-moon days, when Buddhists may choose to visit their nearest monastery

9.5 Other celebrations and festivals

Focusing questions

- Which three events in the life of the Buddha are often celebrated by Buddhists on the same day?
- What do many Buddhists do to mark the day on which the Buddha was enlightened?
- Where does the festival of the Sacred Tooth take place and how is it celebrated?

There is no authority in the Buddhist scriptures for commemorating events in the life of the Buddha. No one knows when Buddhists first began these celebrations.

Events in the life of the Buddha

Celebrating the birth of the Buddha, which in China is thought to be more important than the enlightenment, is an old custom. In Sri Lanka, Burma and Thailand Theravada Buddhists believe that the Buddha's birth, enlightenment and death happened on the same date and so celebrate the events together. The name in India for the month in which the celebration takes place is **Vaisakha**, whilst in Sri Lanka the name **Wesak** is used for both the month and the festival.

In many places, though, it is the enlightenment which is considered to be the most important event and lamps are lit to symbolise the light which replaced the darkness when the Buddha was enlightened. In Burma it is usual to water the bodhi tree, since it was under such a tree that the Buddha achieved enlightenment.

The time when the Buddha first preached the Dharma is a joyous festival in Buddhist countries.

Local festivals and celebrations

In addition to the main festivals there are others which are celebrated locally. Some of these are associated with a relic of the Buddha which is preserved in a particular locality. The best-known example of this is the festival of the Sacred Tooth, which takes place at Kandy in Sri Lanka. The sacred rooth (a relic of the Buddha) is taken from the temple, drums are played and elephants decorated for this most colourful of all Buddhist festivals. The largest of the elephants carries the sacred relic in a miniature stupa (see 6.4). The people who line the route shout, blow conch shells, bang cymbals and create as much noise as they can.

Also in Sri Lanka thousands of Buddhists go to a sacred mountain near to the ancient city of Anuradhapura to recall the first preaching in that country by a monk called Mahinda, the son of Asoka (see 6.4).

Key question Which events in the life of the Buddha are of the greatest significance to Buddhists and how are they remembered?

An early 5th-century traveller found people celebrating the birth of the Buddha in China:

Every year, on the eighth day of the second month, they celebrate a procession of images. They make a four-wheeled car, and on it erect a structure of five storeys by means of bamboos tied together. On the four sides are niches, with a Buddha seated in each, and a bodhisattva standing in attendance on him. There

The sacred tooth relic leaving the temple, Kandy, Sri Lanka may be 20 cars, all grand and imposing, but each one different from the others. Then, on the great day, both monks and lay people come together with singers and musicians, making their devotions with flowers and incense. This goes on for two nights, with lamps burning and music playing all through the nights. Wealthy families dispense charity and give medicines to the poor and the disabled.

☐ Why do you think that the wealthy take this opportunity to dispense charity and medicines to the poor and the disabled?

Work to do
Look carefully at the photograph, which shows Buddhists celebrating the festival of the Sacred Tooth in Sri Lanka.
 (a) How is the sacred tooth carried, and why do you think it is being taken from the temple?
 (b) Why do you think elephants are used to carry the relic?
 (c) Find out about other festivals in which sacred relics are carried through the streets.
 (d) Can you find out more about the festival of the Sacred Tooth?

Key words   **Vaisakha:** (or in Sri Lanka, **Wesak**) festival held on the full moon day of May, celebrating the enlightenment of the Buddha and, in some cases, also his birth and death. Processions are held and various ceremonies performed

9.6 The Buddhist monastery

■ What is a monastic Sangha?
■ How are the monks and nuns in a Sangha supported?
■ What are they expected to do for the community in return?

Monks accepting alms, Bangkok, Thailand

Ever since the time of the Buddha's enlightenment there have been men and women who were prepared to give up everything to find out the meaning of the Four Noble Truths and the Eightfold Path. These people are the monastic Sangha, the community of Buddhist monks, or **bhikkhus**. They are the living link with the Buddha and his teaching. Bhikkhus live in monasteries built by people who also follow the Buddha but who choose to live with their families. These householders also ensure that the monks receive food.

Duties of the householder

The same Buddhist scriptures which lay down rules for the monks also outline the duties of those householders who continue to live at home. The householders are to:

☐ look after their parents;
☐ treat their elders with respect;
☐ use gentle words;
☐ avoid malicious and unpleasant talk;
☐ be generous in everything;
☐ speak the truth at all times;
☐ avoid being angry.

Yet, important as these duties are, they cannot lead any person to enlightenment. The person who really wants to reach nirvana must enter a Sangha and become a monk.

Entering a monastery

A person entering a Buddhist monastery today will find that they have to go through a trial period before being ordained. They will also find that the demands placed upon them are virtually the same as those demanded of monks in the time of the Buddha:

☐ Fine clothes must be avoided. A patched robe must be worn.
☐ Each monk must only eat once a day.
☐ Each monk may only possess that which is placed in their alms bowl by householders. Monks are not allowed to beg.
☐ No monk may handle money.
☐ Each monk must spend part of the year living in the forest.
☐ Whilst in the monastery each monk must restrict the amount of time spent sleeping. He must sit on a carpet, even when asleep, and is not allowed to lie down.

Those who would be Buddhist monks must be prepared to accept the 227 rules which govern the everyday conduct of members of the Sangha. Everything is provided for the monks by members of the community which benefits from the services of the monks. The main service which the monks render to the community is that of teaching the people about the Buddhist way of life.

Key question   **How are Buddhist monks and householders expected to behave?**

The five people who first heard the message of the Buddha were sent out by him with the following commission:

Go ye forth, O monks, for the salvation and joy of many, out of compassion for the world. Go not two together on the same path. Preach, O monks, the doctrine which is noble in its beginnings, in its course, and in its consummation. Proclaim the noble path.

☐ The first monks were given *two* reasons for going out into the world to preach. What were they?
☐ Why do you think that they were told 'Go not two together on the same path'?
☐ What do you think was meant by the words 'Preach . . . the doctrine which is noble in its beginnings, in its course, and in its consummation'?
☐ How do you think these words of the Buddha might be applied to a Buddhist monk in today's world?

> ### Work to do
> **Some of the rules which govern the lives of Buddhist monks are listed above. Can you suggest reasons for *three* of them?**

Key words   **bhikkhu:** Buddhist monk; the word itself means 'almsman' and underlines the poverty of all those who belong to the Sangha

9.7 The life of a Buddhist monk

Focusing questions
- What are the two stages of ordination into the Buddhist monastic order?
- Why does the Buddhist community consider it a privilege to support those living within a monastery?
- What are the two main tasks that members of the Buddhist monastic orders are expected to perform in the community?

In the Theravada tradition of Buddhism there are two stages through which monks and nuns seeking ordination must pass:

☐ As a novice the monk or nun follows the Ten Precepts.
☐ At the age of 20 the monk or nun can pass through a higher ordination.

The robe and the alms bowl

The outward symbol of the devotion of the monk to the teachings of the Buddha is his saffron robe. This is the traditional colour worn in India by those who renounce the world. The robe is a symbol of wisdom, knowledge and concentration. It also symbolises the fact that the monk has discovered the way to be released from the desire that causes all suffering. The Buddhist monk is totally dependent upon the gifts of lay followers for his robe, and for all his food and drink. Ordinary Buddhists are happy to bestow such generosity on the monks since they believe that the presence of bhikkhus as teachers and guardians of the Dharma in the community is very important.

In a Theravada country it is very common to see saffron-robed monks carrying their alms bowls to collect the gifts of the faithful. They do so in silence since they are not allowed to ask the people for food. Ordinary Buddhists must be ready to offer food and, at the same time, to thank the monks for providing them with an opportunity of 'making merit'.

Everyday life

Buddhist monks are only allowed to eat one main meal a day. This means that the rest of the day is free for them to give themselves to meditation, study, teaching the laity, and practical work. In all this they have two main tasks:

☐ They must meditate so that their own enlightenment is brought nearer. In many Buddhist traditions meditation is said to be the main work of the monk.
☐ They must preserve the teachings of the Buddha faithfully and pass them on to the people, to help lead them towards enlightenment.

This does not mean that all Buddhist monks live under the same conditions. There are some monastic communities situated in remote places, such as forests, where the life-style is very simple and meditation is given the highest priority. Other monastic communities are in villages, where most of the time is spent in supervising the local shrines and helping the people in their everyday lives. Yet other monastic groups are dedicated to the writing of books and making sure that the Buddhist tradition is maintained as purely as possible.

Although most Buddhist monks and nuns do live in settled communities there is a custom of trying to shake off attachment to this world by simply walking through the countryside from community to community for weeks, months or even years.

Key question **Why is a Buddhist monk or nun considered to be a very important part of the community?**

This description was written by a British monk who walked for 13 days with a companion to shake off his attachment to the world:

> *When the walk came to an end, 13 mornings after leaving, the practice-path that it symbolises continued: the monastic life is about non-abiding, it is a giving up of personal possessions, desires, concerns and opinions. You listen and live close to the heart of life, and the only refuge from the rawness of our nature is to do good and be mindful. Sometimes that seems to leave you completely alone with nothing to hold on to, but the path evokes a compassion in us that fills the heart, and a respect for our way of life that gives us many friends. Before we reached the monastery, we stopped to say hello to Sam, the woodsman who works in the barn at the top of Chithurst Lane. 'You've just got back, have you?' he said. 'Please, wait a moment.' He walked to the back of his workshop and returned with half of his packed lunch. 'Can I put this into your bowl?'*

☐ What do you think the writer meant when he says, at the end of the walk, 'the practice-path that it symbolises continued'?

☐ What indications are there in this extract that the path chosen by the Buddhist monk is not an easy one?

☐ When the going appears to be hard what does the monk take refuge in?

> ### Work to do
> **Find out as much as you can about monastic life in *one* other major world religion. In what ways is it similar to the life of a Buddhist monk; in what ways is it different?**

9.8 Meditation

Focusing questions
- What does a Buddhist gain through meditation?
- What are the different stages of meditation through which a Buddhist passes?
- What is different about meditation in Zen Buddhism?

Zen master leading a meditation

For Buddhists meditation is a way of helping the mind to settle down into a tranquil state of clarity and openness. Monks, in particular, spend a great deal of time meditating (**samadhi**). By controlling the mind they hope to see the inner reality of the Buddha's teachings.

Meditation fosters feelings of love, compassion and generosity in the person. It turns the mind away from those evil thoughts and false ideas which lie at the heart of all suffering. To meditate properly the help and support of a group is needed. Buddhist monks meditate together under the leadership of a 'meditation master', who gives leadership and directs the minds of everyone towards the object of the meditation.

The stages of meditation

Although different groups may vary slightly, the main stages in Buddhist meditation are well established:

☐ Meditation can take place either inside or outside. Usually a simple object such as a flower is provided to help the mind to concentrate.
☐ Gradually the mind is concentrated on the object to the total exclusion of everything else.
☐ The eyes are closed and the object is visualised in the mind. Gradually the meditator then moves away from the concrete to the abstract.
☐ Next the mind progresses from the effort needed to concentrate to meditation without any effort.
☐ It is in this effortless state that the person experiences inner freedom and a feeling of being in space without any limitations.
☐ Whilst they are in this state those meditating are able to see to the very heart of things, where reality is to be found.

It is not easy for the outsider to appreciate the true nature of meditation since it is very much a technique that one can only really appreciate by personal experience.

Meditation in Zen Buddhism

Zen Buddhism is particularly popular in Japan and this has its own distinctive form of meditation. The master begins by asking a riddle (called a koan). One of the best-known koans is 'What is the sound of one hand clapping?' This riddle cannot be solved by logical reasoning or using the mind. It can only be solved by breaking through to a higher level of reality.

Key question **What is meditation and why is it such an important part of Buddhism?**

The Buddha said:

In the seeing there should be just the seeing, in the hearing just the hearing, and in the thinking just the thought.

☐ What do you think that the Buddha was trying to teach his followers when he said these words?

Work to do

1. This extract is taken from the Pali Canon.
Whether he walk or stand or rest or lie
Or stretch his limbs or draw them in again,
Let him do all these things composedly;
Above, across, and back again returning –
Whatever be one's bourn in all the world –
Let him be one who views the rise-and-fall
Of all the compounded things attentively.
So dwelling ardent, living a life of peace
And not elated, but to calmness given,
For mind's composure doing what is right,
Ever and always training – 'ever intent' –
That is the name men give to such a monk.

(a) One quality, above all others, is looked for in a Buddhist. On the basis of this extract what do you think this quality is?

(b) Meditation is often called the 'work' of the monk, who devotes much time to practising it. How is this reflected in the above extract?

2. Find out as much as you can about meditation. In particular try to answer these questions:

(a) What is unusual about meditation in Zen Buddhism?

(b) What problems might be encountered by a person who wants to meditate regularly in a modern industrial country?

(c) Why do people who are not Buddhists take up meditation to help them to cope with the strains and stresses of life today?

Key words **samadhi:** term used in Buddhism for intense concentration in meditation

10. THE STAGES OF LIFE

10.1 From birth to marriage

Focusing questions

- What are paritta and on what occasions might they be used?
- How might a Buddhist couple celebrate the birth of their baby?
- What is unusual about a Buddhist marriage?
- What part are members of the Sangha expected to play in Buddhist weddings?

Although Buddhist customs connected with birth and marriage vary somewhat from country to country, and between Theravada and Mahayana Buddhism, they often involve members of the Sangha or monastic order.

Birth

Whilst there are no particular Buddhist ceremonies which must be performed at the birth of a baby, monks are often invited into the home to chant **paritta** (texts from Buddhist scriptures). In return for this parents give food or other gifts to the local Sangha.

The child can also be taken along to the temple to be named. At this ceremony a monk sprinkles water over the child before pronouncing a blessing over it, expressing the hope of a happy life to come. The union of the four elements – solidity, fluidity, heat and motion – is also symbolised at this ceremony by burning a pure wax candle and then allowing the molten wax to fall into a bowl of pure water. The coming-together and uniting of the elements symbolises that unity which, it is hoped, the child will achieve throughout its life.

Marriage

In the life of a Buddhist, marriage means that they have left the stage of a student behind and entered on that of a householder. This is a highly respected condition in a Buddhist country since it is the householders who materially support the monks. Householders have their own code of behaviour and are expected to follow the Five Precepts. Yet, according to Theravada Buddhism, it is a stage with limitations. Whilst not impossible, it is extremely unlikely that a person could reach enlightenment from this stage. This is because there are too many worldly distractions available to the householder. The best that he or she can hope for is to win enough merit for a better rebirth.

In most Buddhist communities the marriage ceremony is largely non-religious, although monks are invited into the home of the bride on the morning of the wedding. They are offered a special feast and, in return, recite the paritta to protect the bride and the groom. The monks then return to their monasteries before the wedding ceremony begins. They neither witness nor participate in the ceremony.

Key question How do Buddhists mark the important events of birth and marriage and what religious significance do they attach to each event?

Some Buddhist groups in this country are developing marriage services which combine the religious and non-religious aspects of marriage. This prayer is taken from a service developed by the Samye Ling Buddhist community in Dumfries:

May there ever be goodness, renown, great riches and all life's necessities in their finest forms: great joy, bliss and happiness, strength, good influence, and the very best material life, which is long enduring, free of sickness and wherein all one's wishes are fulfilled.

☐ How do these wishes for a married couple compare with those in the wedding service of one other religion you are familiar with?

Work to do

1. (a) **What might be chanted in a Buddhist home after a baby has been born, and by whom?**
   (b) **What does a monk do at the same time as sprinkling a baby with water?**
   (c) **Which four elements are symbolised by the burning of a wax candle?**
   (d) **Why is the wax from the candle allowed to drop into a bowl of water?**
   (e) **What does the uniting of the four elements symbolise?**

2. (a) **What stage in the life of a Buddhist has been reached when he or she marries?**
   (b) **What code of behaviour is expected of all people who are married?**
   (c) **Why is it unlikely that a person could reach enlightenment from the householder stage?**
   (d) **What happens on the morning of most Buddhist weddings?**

Key words **paritta:** texts from the Buddhist scriptures which are used to keep worshippers from danger

10.2 Pilgrimage

Focusing questions

- Which four places of pilgrimage did Gautama Buddha recommend his followers to visit?
- Why might it be beneficial for a Buddhist to visit these, or any of the other places of pilgrimage?

Towards the end of his life Gautama Buddha recommended that his followers should visit four places:

- ☐ his birth-place;
- ☐ the place at which he became enlightened;
- ☐ the place in which he preached his first sermon;
- ☐ the place where he was to die.

Visiting the holy places

Gautama Buddha was born in Kapilavastu, which is in modern Nepal. He was enlightened at Bodh Gaya in Bihar in India and he preached his first sermon ('Turning the Wheel of the Dharma') in Sarnath, which is now on the outskirts of Benares in the state of Uttar Pradesh. No one, however, is sure of the place where Gautama Buddha died.

It is not obligatory for Buddhists to visit any of the many pilgrimage sites. If visited, however, all of them can bring a close sense of fellowship between Buddhists and a deeper understanding of the religious faith an individual belongs to. Until comparatively recently most of the sites were in an advanced state of disrepair – the most important of those which have been restored is Bodh Gaya, where pilgrims will find a large statue of the Buddha at the time when he was enlightened. Today the temple at Bodh Gaya (the Mahabodhi Temple) is thought by many Buddhists to have considerable spiritual power, brought about largely

Pilgrims offering flowers and incense at the Bodh Gaya temple in India

by the immense number of pilgrims who visit it every year. Those who visit the temple offer flowers, incense and light, and sit in silent meditation beneath the bodhi tree. They also hang coloured prayer flags on the tree so that they can leave their prayers behind them.

Among the other pilgrimage sites are many places in Japan, Sri Lanka and Tibet which draw pilgrims to find physical and spiritual refreshment. To Buddhists a pilgrimage becomes any journey, internal or external, that is taken for the purpose of finding spiritual refreshment.

Key question   **Which places are particularly holy for all Buddhists, and why?**

An extract from the *Mahaparinirvana Sutra*:

> *There are four places, Ananda, which the devoted person should visit with feelings of reverence. What are the four? The place, Ananda, at which the devoted person can say: 'Here the Buddha was born!' is a spot to be visited with feelings of reverence.*
>
> *The place, Ananda, at which the devoted person can say: 'Here the Buddha attained to supreme and highest wisdom!' is a spot to be visited with feelings of reverence.*
>
> *The place, Ananda, at which the devoted person can say, 'Here the Wheel of the Dharma was set in motion by the Buddha!' is a spot to be visited with feelings of reverence.*
>
> *The place, Ananda, at which the devoted person can say, 'Here the Buddha passed finally away' is a spot to be visited with feelings of reverence.*

☐ What do you think that the word 'reverence' means and why is each holy place to be visited in this frame of mind?

Work to do
These two extracts are taken from the BBC radio programme *Worlds of Faith*.

1. *For us, a pilgrimage is to hear a lecture – as a pilgrimage, to hear the Dalai Lama, to hear some eminent Buddhist scholar. It's not just listening to a lecture, but a pilgrimage, because in Buddhism we talk all the time about the transmission of the Dharma; and the transmission for us is not just a talking, or a communication, but almost a literal, physical, passing across.*
  (a) Do you know who the Dalai Lama is? If not, find out.
  (b) What is a pilgrimage to this speaker and what is important about every such journey?

2. *When I was even a boy, we were taken to Nepal, where Lord Buddha was born. Near Nepal, there were two very high temples . . . I don't know when they were constructed, I can't remember; but they were very famous. So we go there for a pilgrimage and we go there with full conviction, with no money – we just go very simply.*
  (a) What do you think the speaker means by the words 'we just go very simply'?
  (b) Why do you think that every religion expects pilgrims to make their journey simply?

10.3 Death

Focusing questions

- What does Buddhism teach about life which enables a Buddhist to accept death calmly?
- How can a person affect their own karma and how can the relatives of a dead person hope to affect their karma?
- What happens if the person who has died is believed to have reached nirvana?

In one sense a Buddhist finds death easier to accept than the follower of any other religion. Throughout his or her life a Buddhist has lived by the principle that all things are impermanent and that decay is always at work. From moment to moment we are all dying. When the time to die actually arrives, therefore, the only attitude a Buddhist can adopt is one of acceptance.

Cremating and remembering

Buddhists believe that people are reborn in the next life according to their karma in this life. Karma is the idea that nothing is ever wasted, that all thoughts, words and deeds bear fruit. The good actions bear good fruit and the bad actions bear bad fruit. We all reap what we sow and this process goes on through the chain of lives.

In the next life a person returns to one of five (or six) realms of existence: the realm of the gods, the human realm, the animal realm, the realm of the 'hungry ghosts' (shown as figures with huge bellies and tiny mouths, which signify their enormous, insatiable appetites), and hell. However, if a person has been enlightened, they can be released to nirvana. The state of mind with which a person faces the last minutes of their present life is very important in determining their karma. Friends, relations and monks gather around the death-bed of the person to engage them in acts of devotion and the recitation of the scriptures.

Monks are involved in the rituals associated with death and the various ceremonies that follow. The rituals that precede burial or cremation may take three days and during this time the monks take the opportunity to remind everyone of the impermanence of life and the hope that eventually everyone will reach the blessed state of nirvana. The relatives and friends of the dead person try to influence their progress towards nirvana by making acts of **dana** (alms giving).

Other important ceremonies take place after the cremation or burial. Held after seven days, three months and annually, these ceremonies are an attempt to transfer some real merit to the dead person. The relatives try to do this by feeding the monks, giving them new robes and taking part in ceremonial water-washing ceremonies.

If the person who has died is believed to have reached nirvana through becoming enlightened or is an **arhant** (saint), relics of the person are collected together after the cremation. These relics can then be placed in a stupa or in a **Buddha-rupa** (statue of the Buddha). When a Buddhist comes across a stupa or sees a Buddha-rupa in a temple or a house he is reminded of the **Buddha-Dharma**.

Key question How is the Buddhist attitude towards death reflected in the rituals and ceremonies which follow the death of a person?

An extract from the *Dharmapada*:

Death carries off a man who is gathering life's flowers, whose mind is distracted, even as a flood carries off a sleeping village.
   All created things are impermanent. When one by wisdom realises this, he heeds not this world of sorrow.

☐ What do you think Gautama Buddha meant when he likened death to the carrying-off of a man who is gathering life's flowers with a distracted mind?

☐ What happens when a person realises that all created things are impermanent?

Work to do

1. In this photograph a Buddhist cremation is about to take place.
   (a) How might the relatives and friends present try to influence the passage of a dead person towards nirvana?
   (b) What might a Buddhist hope for this person being cremated?
   (c) What happens to the relics of dead saints and those believed to have been enlightened?

Awaiting cremation at the Bodh Gaya temple in India

2. Hindus have cremation ceremonies which are in many ways similar to those of Buddhists. Find out from section 5.5 the similarities and differences.

Key words   **arhant:** a saint, one who has followed the Eightfold Path and has reached nirvana
Buddha-Dharma: the teaching of the Buddha
Buddha-rupa: image or statue of the Buddha
dana: term used in Buddhism for the virtue of giving alms to the poor and needy and to the bhikkus

PART 3

SIKHISM

11. THE ORIGINS OF SIKHISM

11.1 Who is a Sikh?

Focusing questions
- How and where did Sikhism start?
- What is a Sikh?
- Where are the majority of Sikhs to be found today?

Sikhism is one of the youngest of the major world religions. It started towards the end of the 15th century in the area of what is now Pakistan and north-west India called the Punjab ('the land of the five rivers'). At that time the Punjab was ruled by Muslims. The founder of Sikhism was **Guru Nanak**, who was born a Hindu. He did not, however, grow up to follow the customs and rituals of Hinduism. Although Guru Nanak retained throughout his life a warm affection for the religion of his birth, he was dissatisfied with its doctrine and practices and taught his small group of disciples that there is but one God and that all people, of whatever religion, are equal in God's sight. You will find out more about Guru Nanak in 11.2.

What is a Sikh?

Originally the word 'Sikh' meant 'a disciple'. The **Sikh Gurdwara Act** of 1925 defined a Sikh as 'one who believes in the ten Gurus and the *Granth Sahib* [*Guru Granth Sahib*] and is not a 'patit' [a lapsed member]'. As there was still some confusion, a meeting was held at **Amritsar** in 1931 to draw up a code which would define true Sikh belief and practice. This gathering defined a true Sikh as someone who:

- [ ] has faith in the one God, the teachings of the ten Gurus and the *Adi Granth*;
- [ ] believes in the necessity and importance of **amrit**;
- [ ] does not belong to any other religion;
- [ ] belongs to a Sikh community and accepts the discipline of that community.

Although Sikhs are now found throughout the world, their faith is still part of an Indian tradition which stresses the importance of personal appearance and hygiene in the service of God. Sikhs wear **turbans** and the **five Ks** (see 14.3) as visible signs of their faith. Almost all acts of worship are preceded by bathing, an act which expresses the Sikh belief that only those people who are physically clean can enter into God's presence.

When Sikhs enter a **gurdwara** (temple) they remove their shoes as a mark of respect for God, whose presence is symbolised by the holy book, the *Guru Granth Sahib*. Even to carry one's shoes through the gurdwara is taken to be an insult to the holy book.

Key question What is distinctive about a Sikh?

Sikhs celebrating Guru Nanak's birthday

Work to do
The map shows the Indian state of Punjab, in which most of the world's Sikhs live. Try to find out as much as you can about this part of India. In particular, find out what happened to the Punjab in 1947.

Key words   **Adi Granth:** first name for holy writings of Sikhism, later known as *Guru Granth Sahib*

amrit: sugared water used at many Sikh ceremonies

Amritsar: the sacred city of the Sikhs, located in the Punjab

five Ks: symbols of faith worn by strict Sikhs: uncut hair, a comb, a wristlet, a sword and shorts

gurdwara: Sikh building used for worship

Guru Granth Sahib: the holy book of the Sikh religion, another name for it is *Adi Granth*

Guru Nanak: (1469–1539) the first Sikh Guru and founder of the Sikh religion

Sikh Gurdwara Act: act passed in 1925 by British government, it returned the management of **gurdwaras** (with their considerable assets) to the Sikhs – they had been in the control of Hindu 'caretakers'. This was an important act because of its definition, for the first time, of Sikhism, and because it listed Sikh shrines

Sikhism: religion based on the teachings of Guru Nanak and the nine other Gurus

turban: traditional male Sikh head-covering

11.2 Guru Nanak

Focusing questions

- ■ How did Guru Nanak receive his call to preach about God?
- ■ What was distinctive about the message preached by Guru Nanak?
- ■ How did Guru Nanak live his life after the age of 30?

Guru Nanak was born in 1469 at Talwindi (now called Nankana Sahib), which is a small town about 50 miles to the south-west of Lahore in modern Pakistan. He belonged to a reasonably prosperous Hindu family, and he soon began to display qualities of wisdom and spiritual insight that marked him out from the other children. His teachers discovered that they had nothing to teach him and he seems to have spent much of his early life talking to travelling holy men about the religions of Islam and Hinduism.

When he was 18 years old, Guru Nanak's father arranged his marriage but when his first son was born he refused to carry out the usual Hindu ceremony to purify the house. Birth, he said, is a natural event and the only impurity is 'the covetous mind, tongues speaking untruths, eyes full of lust, and ears accepting unreliable evidence as true'.

For 14 years Guru Nanak served the provincial governor as a storekeeper, but gradually an interest in spiritual matters began to take over. He spent most of his leisure time in meditation and solitude.

Receiving the call

Then, at the age of 30, he had a remarkable spiritual experience which changed the whole course of his life. Whilst he was bathing in the River Bein near Sultanpur he felt himself being carried up into the divine court to appear before God. Once there he was given a cup of nectar (amrit) to drink, and God then spoke to him. The people back home were convinced that he had drowned, but Guru Nanak returned to the earth after three days. He remained silent for a

Guru Nanak

further day before telling the people the message that he had been given. God, he told the people, had called him to be a **guru**. For the next 20 years he travelled through India and the adjoining Muslim countries visiting all the holy places of Hinduism and Islam, talking to the religious leaders. Then, in later life, he settled down as a farmer in the Punjab with his family. Gradually a community of disciples grew up around him there. A few days before his death in 1539, Guru Nanak nominated his most devoted disciple to succeed him.

The message

The message that Guru Nanak preached to the people was very clear and in many ways it cut across their Hindu or Muslim beliefs. He told them that:

☐ there is one God who is both present with them in the world and yet over and above that world;

☐ there is a continual cycle of birth, life, death and rebirth;

☐ the goal of every person's soul is to be eventually absorbed into God;

☐ those who hope to be absorbed into God must discipline themselves and live their lives by following certain moral principles. Above all else, they must live their lives in humility, in the service of others.

Key question **What religious experience did Guru Nanak undergo and what was the basis of the message that he passed on to the people from God?**

This is an extract from the *Guru Granth Sahib*:

> *I was a minstrel out of work.*
> *The Lord gave me employment,*
> *The Mighty One instructed me, 'Night and day, sing my praise.'*
> *The Lord summoned the minstrel*
> *To his High Court.*
> *On me he bestowed the robe of honouring him and singing*
> *   his praise.*
> *On me he bestowed the nectar in a cup,*
> *The nectar of his true and holy name*

☐ Who was the 'minstrel' and why was this name appropriate?

☐ How did the Lord summon the minstrel to his High Court?

☐ What was the 'nectar' that the minstrel drank?

☐ How did the minstrel set out to honour God?

Work to do

There is neither Hindu nor Muslim so whose path shall I follow? I shall follow God's path. God is neither Hindu nor Muslim and the path which I follow is God's.

(a) Who spoke these words and who was he speaking to?

(b) Why were these words particularly surprising to those who first heard them?

To answer this fully, you need to find out what was happening in India at the time of Guru Nanak's life.

Key words **guru:** holy man or teacher in an Indian religion

11.3 The Sikh Gurus

Focusing questions

- What was the great contribution made by Guru Angad to the growth of Sikhism?
- What is the 'langar' and why was it introduced into Sikh community life?
- How was the town of Amritsar founded and who built the Golden Temple there?

Guru Nanak had two sons and they were not very pleased to learn that their father had chosen a follower, Lehna, to carry on his work instead of them. Many times, however, Guru Nanak had asked his sons to carry out tasks for him and they had refused since they considered the work to be beneath their dignity. Lehna, however, had obeyed at once and, by so doing, had shown himself to be the best person to take up the leadership. So Lehna became Guru Angad. All of the Gurus that succeeded Guru Angad were chosen for similar reasons.

Guru Angad (1539–52) is credited with developing **Gurmukhi** – the script in which the Sikh scriptures were written. He did this by combining the two scripts of Devanagri and Lande. To teach this new form of writing to the children, Guru Angad opened a school. Gurmukhi was very important in the growth of Sikhism since it meant that the new religion could break away from Hinduism and forge a clear identity of its own. Soon hymns were written in Gurmukhi with the name 'Nanak' always appearing in the last line.

Guru Amar Das (1552–74) discovered that when people had visited Guru Nanak they always sat down and ate together. This was not the custom amongst most Muslims or Hindus, but it was a means of teaching the all-important lesson that all people are equal in God's sight. To reinforce this, Guru Amar Das built the **langar**, or open kitchen, so that everyone who wanted to visit the Guru could sit down and eat a meal first. Guru Amar Das also protested against the Muslim custom of **purdah** since everyone, male and female, was equal before God. The remaining Gurus were all members of his family.

The fourth Guru, Guru Amar Das's son-in-law, Ram Das (1574–81), is best known for founding the holy city of Amritsar. The land on which the city stands was given to the Sikhs by a Muslim emperor, Akbar, and the foundation stone was laid in 1577. Guru Ram Das also composed the wedding hymns, which meant that Sikhs marrying were no longer compelled to use the Hindu scriptures and priests.

The son of Guru Ram Das, Guru Arjan (1581–1606), was the first Guru to be born as a Sikh. He built a beautiful temple (the 'Harimandir' or 'house of God') in the middle of an artificial lake in Amritsar. Later this building became known as the Golden Temple. Guru Arjan was also instrumental in gathering together the hymns written by the earlier Gurus, adding some of his own, and publishing them as the *Adi Granth* (first book). This was later to be known as the *Guru Granth Sahib*.

With the death of the Indian emperor, Akbar, in 1605, the religious climate in the country changed. Although he had been a Muslim, Akbar had respected the Sikh Gurus. In the following year Guru Arjan became the first Sikh martyr when he died whilst in custody. From now on Sikhs showed themselves willing to take up the sword, if necessary, to defend their religious faith.

During the time of the sixth Guru, Guru Hargobind (1606–44), the persecution increased. Guru Hargobind taught the Sikhs that they must be prepared to fight for their faith, but he also cared greatly for their spiritual life. For this reason he carried two swords – one the symbol of battle and the other of the spirit. He spent some years imprisoned in the Gwalior fort.

The ninth Guru, Tegh Bahadur (1664–75), also died for his faith, choosing death rather than Islam (see 11.4).

By the time of Guru Gobind Singh (1675–1708), the tenth Guru, the recent history of the Sikhs had been one of torture, repression and death. It was necessary to build the faith into a fighting force so that it could defend itself. It was for this reason that Guru Gobind Singh formed the **Khalsa**, the brotherhood of Sikhs, in 1699. You will discover how he did this, and the principles on which the Khalsa is based, in 11.4.

Key question **What contributions to the growth and development of Sikhism were made by the various Sikh Gurus?**

Work to do

1. Write down *three* pieces of information about each of these Gurus:
   (a) Guru Angad (b) Guru Ram Das (c) Guru Hargobind (d) Guru Gobind Singh.

2. This picture shows Guru Gobind Singh. Are there any clues in the picture to suggest the contribution that he made to Sikhism?

Key words **Gurmukhi:** the script in which the Sikh scriptures were written
Khalsa: the Sikh brotherhood, founded by Guru Gobind Singh in 1699
langar: kitchen attached to a Sikh gurdwara where a communal meal is eaten after worship
purdah: Persian word for 'veil'; refers to the garment which many Muslim women wear in public to conceal them from the outside world

11.4 The Khalsa brotherhood

Focusing questions
- Why was the Khalsa formed?
- Who were the Panj Pyare and how were they singled out from other Sikhs?
- What standards of discipline were demanded from the early members of the Khalsa and all those who have joined since?

During the 17th century the rulers of India were forcing people to become Muslims. A group of Hindus turned to Guru Tegh Bahadur, the ninth Guru, for help to save Hinduism. Accompanied by several of his supporters, the Guru travelled to the Muslim court in the city of Delhi to ask the authorities to stop the persecution. For their trouble they were thrown into prison and told that they would be killed if they did not submit to Islam. They chose to die rather than renounce their faith, and so were executed.

The Faithful Ones

Guru Gobind Rai succeeded Guru Tegh Bahadur, to become the tenth and last Guru. The persecution of the Sikhs by the Muslims continued, so Guru Gobind Rai called all Sikhs together for the April festival of Baisakhi. He asked the large assembly for volunteers who would be prepared to die for their faith. He made the request with a drawn sword in his hand. After a long silence one man went into the Guru's tent. The Guru reappeared alone with a bloodstained sword. Four more men followed into the tent before the five (the **Panj Pyare** as they are now called) emerged with the Guru. All Sikhs pay tribute to the fearless courage of the five men – the Faithful Ones. The five Faithful Ones formed the nucleus of the Khalsa ('the Pure'). They were given nectar (amrit) made from water and sugar crystals which was prepared in an iron bowl and stirred with a two-edged sword (khanda, see 14.1) before the Guru himself received the same initiation.

The code of discipline

Guru Gobind Rai laid down a strict code of discipline for those Sikhs who wanted to become members of the Khalsa: no tobacco; no eating of animals already slaughtered according to the laws of the Muslim tradition; no sexual intercourse with Muslim women; no contact with any people who were challenging the authority of the Sikh leaders.

In addition all members of the Khalsa were to display proudly, the five symbols (the five Ks): uncut hair; a comb; a steel wristlet; a sword; short breeches or trousers.

Men who became members of the Khalsa were to take on the surname 'Singh' (lion), so Guru Gobind Rai became Guru Gobind Singh. Women were also allowed to join and they took the surname 'Kaur' (princess).

Soon the number of Sikhs who had received their 'baptism by the sword' grew considerably and the Khalsa has remained the focus of the unity between Sikhs ever since.

The ideals of the Khalsa are very precious to its members. All decisions are made by the brotherhood in the presence of the *Guru Granth Sahib*. Guru Gobind Singh said that the *Guru Granth Sahib* would be the '11th Guru' (the final Guru).

Key question Why was it necessary to form the Khalsa and what was it dedicated to?

Requirements of the Khalsa from Guru Gobind Singh:

He who repeats night and day the name of God whose enduring light is unquenchable. He who bestows not a thought on any but the one God. He who has full love and confidence in God and who places no faith, even by mistake, in fasting, worshipping at tombs, places of cremation or at places where yogis meditate. He who recognises only the one God and cares not for pilgrimages, alms, penances and austerities.

In whose heart the light of the perfect one shines, he is recognised as a pure member of the Khalsa.

☐ Several religious activities are mentioned here and condemned. What are they?
☐ How can a pure member of the Khalsa be recognised?

The first amrit ceremony

Work to do

1. Look carefully at this picture. It shows the first amrit ceremony with two dead hawks lying on their backs whilst the two doves who have killed them are perched on the bowl of nectar. What do you think that this picture symbolises?

2. Carry out some research of your own to find out more about the five Ks. In particular, try to find answers to the following questions:
   (a) What does the uncut hair (kesh) symbolise?
   (b) What practical use does the comb (kangha) have?
   (c) What does the sword (kirpan) symbolise?
   (d) What kind of necessary protection was originally offered by the steel bracelet (the kara)?
   (e) Why are members of the Khalsa expected to wear shorts (kaccha)?

Key words   **Panj Pyare:** the five companions of Guru Gobind Singh when the Khalsa was first formed in 1699

11.5 The spread of Sikhism

Focusing questions

- How did Guru Gobind Singh indicate what was to succeed him as the Guru of the Sikhs?
- What was installed as the Guru after the death of Guru Gobind Singh in 1708?
- What was the major event in the 20th century which changed the history of Sikhism?

When Guru Gobind Singh died in 1708 the Sikhs no longer had a human Guru to guide them. Just before his death Guru Gobind Singh is said to have taken five coins and a coconut, placed them in front of the *Granth Sahib* and installed it as Guru. From this moment on, any building which contained a copy of the *Guru Granth Sahib* became a gurdwara and a building in which the worship of God could take place. The same remains true today.

The Sikh faith under siege

Soon after the death of Guru Gobind Singh, Sikhs were involved in a revolt against the Muslim Mogul rulers in the Punjab. When many Sikhs were killed in the fighting it became clear that armed resistance would be needed to preserve the future of the faith. This fighting could only be justified, however, if it was allied with a faithful keeping of the most important Sikh practices. A continual reading of the *Guru Granth Sahib* (called the **Akhand Path**) was found to be particularly useful in sustaining small groups of Sikh soldiers in battle.

Internal challenges

With the decline of the Moguls the Sikhs were able to bring most of the Punjab under their control by the end of the 18th century. Gradually new leaders emerged. One of these was Ranjit Singh, who took the city of Lahore and set up his capital there. He was able to build many gurdwaras and restore the Golden Temple but the Sikh faith faced two internal challenges:

☐ Many of the Sikhs went back to their old Hindu practices.
☐ Several Sikh sects sprang up, weakening the position of those who were trying to remain loyal to the teachings of the ten Gurus.

When, in 1925, the Sikh Gurdwara Act was passed (see 11.1) it placed the responsibility for looking after Sikh shrines in the hands of a committee. This committee soon decided that true Sikhism had been diluted for many years by the close links that people had maintained with Hinduism. The committee led a movement back to 'pure' Sikhism by defining a genuine Sikh as 'one who believes in the ten Gurus and the *Granth Sahib*'.

Sikhism as a world religion

In 1947 the Sikh homeland, the Punjab, was divided and some 2,600,000 Sikhs moved into India from that part of the Punjab which was now controlled by Pakistan. In many ways this was very important for the future of Sikhism. Although 80 per cent of the world's Sikhs still live in the Punjab, Sikhs began to see their faith as a world religion, not just a local one. Many Sikhs left their homeland to settle in the USA and Britain. Almost 250,000 now live in North America (the USA and Canada), whilst around 400,000 have made their homes in Britain. You will find out much more about this community, the largest outside the Punjab, in 11.6.

Key question How has the Sikh religion spread since its origins in the Punjab during the 16th and 17th centuries?

> *Work to do*
>
> 1. In 1984 a very important event in Sikh history took place. Sikhs had been trying to win greater independence from Indian control in the Punjab and, as a result, Indian soldiers invaded the Golden Temple at Amritsar.
>
> Carry out your own research to find out the details of this episode and the important impact that it had upon the Sikh community. Try to answer these questions:
>
> (a) What was the name of the Indian Prime Minister who ordered Indian troops into the Golden Temple? What happened to her on 31 October 1984 and who is thought to have been responsible?
>
> (b) Which Sikh religious leader became the focus for opposition to the Indians? What did he set up in the Golden Temple complex? What happened to him and many of his followers in the end?
>
> (c) What did some Sikhs want to set up?
>
> (d) What was the impact of the 'Golden Temple' incident on Sikhs throughout the world?
>
> 2. Find out as much as you can about the partition of India in 1947.
>
> 3. Draw up your own time chart to show the main events in the history of Sikhism.

Key words **Akhand Path:** continual reading of the *Guru Granth Sahib*, the Sikh holy book, which takes about 48 hours

11.6 The Sikh community in Britain

Focusing questions

■ When and for what reason did Sikhs start coming to Britain in large numbers?
■ Where are the main Sikh communities to be found in Britain?

Sikh travel agent

As we discovered in 11.5, the most sizeable Sikh community outside the Punjab is found in Britain. Although the first gurdwara in the country was opened in 1911, in Putney, the majority of Sikhs came to Britain in the 1950s and early 1960s. They came to Britain looking for work and prosperity, attracted by advertisements placed by companies such as London Transport. Often families were left behind while fathers found work and a place to live. Then, in the 1960s, women and children came, to form a community which now numbers around 400,000.

Although most of the Sikhs who settled in Britain came from the Punjab, a large number also came from such East African countries as Uganda. The vast majority settled in or around the largest industrial cities. Sikh communities can be found in:

☐ London – especially Southall;
☐ Birmingham, Walsall, Solihull and other surrounding towns;
☐ Leicester and other Midland towns;
☐ West Yorkshire – especially Leeds, Bradford and Huddersfield.

The Sikhs settled in these areas because these were places where there was a considerable shortage of labour in certain occupations. Sikhs have become businessmen, shopkeepers, labourers and bus-drivers, as well as owning their own shops, warehouses, garages and offices.

To meet the religious and social needs of this widespread community over 100 gurdwaras have been opened. As well as providing a spiritual focus for the community, they are also centres where Sikhs can meet and learn more of their own customs, traditions and language.

The problems of the Sikh community

In their search for work in the 1960s, many Sikhs were prepared to discard those elements which marked them out as distinctive – their uncut hair, turbans and beards – if they were able to find a job as a result. For a Sikh these were considerable sacrifices to make and they are, thankfully, rarely required to do the same today.

During the 1970s the Sikh community and the law came into conflict when new legislation compelled all motor-cyclists to wear crash helmets. This would have meant that Sikhs would have to remove their turbans and, after much protest, they were exempted from the law.

There has been some tension between the different generations in the Sikh community over marriage customs. Traditionally Sikh marriages are **arranged marriages**. This can cause problems in families where there are young people who prefer to follow Western customs. Following this tradition does mean, however, that the Sikh way of life and Sikh values will be conserved (see 16.3).

The British Sikh community has also been in some difficulty over the disposal of dead bodies. In the Punjab a body is normally burnt and the ashes scattered over the waters of the nearest river. This is not allowed in Britain, so arrangements have been made for ashes to be scattered on the open sea, although some caskets are still flown to the Punjab.

As far as the future is concerned, one problem to be faced is whether Sikh worship will continue to be conducted in the traditional Sikh language, Punjabi, or whether communities will switch to English. Certainly fewer and fewer Sikhs are learning the language of their ancestors (Punjabi). Perhaps the preaching and teaching in the gurdwara in future will have to be bilingual.

Key question   **In what ways does the Sikh community in Britain maintain its social and religious identity. In what ways does living in Britain make this difficult?**

Work to do
1. **Invite a representative of the Sikh community in to speak to your class. Try to find out the answers to these, and many other, questions.**
   (a) How important are the teachings of Guru Nanak and the other Gurus to Sikhs?
   (b) What are the main aspects of those teachings?
   (c) How strong is the Sikh religion in the world today?
   (d) How strong is the Sikh community in Britain and what particular problems does it face?
   (e) What does the future hold for the Sikh religion?

2. **Carry out some research of your own and then write 250 words about 'Being a Sikh in Britain today'.**

Key words   **arranged marriage:** marriage for which parents choose the partner for their son or daughter

12. THE SIKH SCRIPTURES

12.1 The *Guru Granth Sahib*

Focusing questions

- What replaced the presence of a living Guru on earth?
- Where is the original *Guru Granth Sahib?*
- Why is the Japji so important?

The death of Guru Gobind Singh brought to an end the line of human Gurus who would teach and guide Sikh believers. Instead, as Guru Gobind told them before he died, all Sikhs would be guided by the words of the Gurus, which had been written down and collected into the *Guru Granth Sahib*. The original name for this book, the *Adi Granth* ('that which is first and original'), indicates clearly its importance in all matters relating to Sikh faith and worship.

The importance of the *Guru Granth Sahib*

The original version of this holy book is an anthology which was compiled by the fifth Guru, Guru Arjan. The physical task of writing out the volume was carried out by Bhai Gurdas Bhalla, who completed it in 1604. The book was then placed in the **Harimandir**, the Golden Temple, at Amritsar. It was the last Guru, Guru Gobind Singh, who then enthroned the book as the sole Guru.

The *Guru Granth Sahib* is a very large collection (1,430 pages) of poems, or hymns, which are placed in the 31 divisions, or melodies, in which they are intended to be sung. Each division begins with the **Mul Mantra**, which is sung at morning and evening services in the gurdwara.

The vast majority of the hymns were written by the different Gurus. The major contributor is Guru Arjan, who has 2,218 hymns to his credit, followed by Guru Nanak (974 hymns) and Guru Amar Das (907 hymns). The holy book also contains hymns written by 36 other holy men from different castes and different parts of India. These include Hindus and Muslims. One Muslim, the poet Kabir, for instance, has contributed 541 hymns. When Sikhs bow in front of the *Guru Granth Sahib*, therefore, they are recognising the wisdom that has been passed down by God through the followers of other religions as well as their own.

The teachings of the *Guru Granth Sahib*

The key to the *Guru Granth Sahib*, and all Sikh teaching, is the **Japji**. Situated in the first section of the *Guru Granth Sahib*, this poem was written by Guru Nanak towards the end of his life. It is the only hymn in the *Granth* that is recited and not sung. You can find a short quotation from it opposite.

There is a strong Sikh tradition that the teaching of one Guru reflected that of all the others – their forms changed but their 'lights merged' and the Guru's spirit remained the same. That same spirit came, then, to inhabit the *Guru Granth Sahib*. This gave to the holy book a unity which can be seen in its teaching:

☐ There is but one God who is Truth.
☐ There is a cycle of rebirth with the form that the next birth takes being determined by karma.
☐ Salvation can only be reached after a person meditates on God, repeats God's name and then serves other people. God helps people by providing them with the teachings of the ten Gurus and the *Guru Granth Sahib*.

☐ All people, male and female, are equal in the sight of God. Each person must work honestly, worship regularly in the gurdwara and give a tithe (one-tenth of their income) to aid the poor.

Key question **What are the main teachings of the *Guru Granth Sahib*? What is meant by the 'spirit' that Sikhs believe inhabits it?**

The Japji

So pure is God's name,
Whoever obeys God knows the pleasure of it in his own heart.
When the hands and the feet are covered in dirt,
You remove it by washing with water.
When the clothes are dirty,
You clean them by washing with soap.
So when the mind is defiled by sin,
It is cleansed by the love of God's Name.

☐ What is it that dirties the body and what defiles the mind?
☐ Why does this extract draw a parallel between washing dirt off the body and purifying the mind?

Work to do

1. If you visit a gurdwara you will see a copy of the Sikh holy book.
   (a) What is the full name of this book and what does the name mean?
   (b) What language is this book written in?
   (c) What are *four* of the main teachings found in this book?
   (d) The Sikh holy book has been called the 'final and immortal Guru'. What do you think that this phrase means?

2. Although translations of the *Guru Granth Sahib* are available, only copies in the original language are used in religious services. Can you suggest *two* reasons for this?

3. Can you find out *two* ways in which the Sikh community treats men and women as equal?

Key words **Harimandir:** the Golden Temple of Amritsar; literally 'abode of the Lord'. The most important of all Sikh temples
Japji: literally 'recitation', the only hymn in the *Guru Granth Sahib* which is recited rather than sung; written by Guru Nanak
Mul Mantra: first words of the *Guru Granth Sahib*

12.2 The *Guru Granth Sahib* in the Sikh community

Focusing questions

■ What does the *Guru Granth Sahib* represent in each gurdwara?

■ What position of honour is reserved for the *Guru Granth Sahib* and what does this symbolise in a gurdwara?

■ What are the four important occasions on which passages from the *Guru Granth Sahib* are read?

The essential spirit that passed on from one Guru to another finally came to rest on the *Guru Granth Sahib*. It is the same spirit that is treated with great respect by all Sikhs. The holy book is thus treated as if it were a living Guru. Each gurdwara is arranged along the lines of the court of an Indian emperor with the *Guru Granth Sahib* occupying a throne below the canopy.

Respecting the holy book

As soon as Guru Gobind Singh had completed the *Guru Granth Sahib* in 1708, he announced that the finished book would be the next, and last, Sikh Guru. Although it was not to be worshipped as such, it would become the visible symbol of God's presence with his people. Its contents could not be changed. It

A British gurdwara

would always have the same number of pages and be written in the same language (Gurmukhi).

The *Guru Granth Sahib* must be treated with the greatest possible courtesy and respect by being housed, if possible, in a room of its own. It is then brought out with great dignity and care, being carried above the heads of the people. It is placed in an elevated position where everyone can see it and opened with a prayer before any act of worship can begin.

In many gurdwaras an official called a **granthi** makes sure that the holy book is draped with embroidered cloths until it is opened. Then it is protected, and shown respect, by being fanned with a whisk of yak hair (a 'chauri'). Should the holy book need to be moved, it is again carried on the head and preceded by a man who scatters holy water in its path. Before this happens, however, a warning is given to the congregation so that they can cover their heads as a sign of respect. Finally, as the *Guru Granth Sahib* is not read at night, it is 'put to bed' with night prayers called **Kirtan Sohilla**.

Use of the *Guru Granth Sahib*

The *Guru Granth Sahib* is used by the Sikh community to symbolise God's presence at the most important stages in a person's life. It is read:

☐ when a baby is named;
☐ when a person is initiated into the Khalsa;
☐ when two Sikhs are married;
☐ when a death has taken place. A continual reading of the *Guru Granth Sahib* brings consolation to the relatives and others who mourn.

Although most copies of the *Guru Granth Sahib* are to be found housed in gurdwaras, individual Sikhs may have a copy of the holy book in their own homes. If they do, it must be treated with the same respect as it is in the gurdwara, and is often housed in a room of its own.

Key question

In what ways do Sikhs show respect for their holy scriptures and why is this respect so important?

Work to do
Look at the photograph opposite carefully:
(a) Where do you think the *Guru Granth Sahib* is located in this gurdwara?
(b) Why is the holy book given such a place of honour?
(c) What is it usually covered with?
(d) What is waved over the *Guru Granth Sahib*, and why?
(e) What is the link between the *Guru Granth Sahib* and the Gurus of the past?
(f) What part does the *Guru Granth Sahib* play in the lives of the Sikh community?

Key words   **granthi:** official of the gurdwara; he is given special responsibility for looking after the Guru Granth Sahib
Kirtan: devotional songs sung during public worship in the gurdwara
Sohilla: the final prayer of the day, recited before going to bed

12.3 The *Dasam Granth*

Focusing questions

- How did the *Dasam Granth* come to be written?
- What kind of material is found in the *Dasam Granth*?
- What is the 'Jap' and why does it play an important part in the devotional lives of many Sikhs?

Although the *Dasam Granth* does not have the status or influence of the *Guru Granth Sahib* within the Sikh community, this book does play an important role in the devotions of many Sikhs. When the tenth Guru, Gobind Singh, added many poems by his father to the *Guru Granth Sahib*, he did not include any of his own. Yet Guru Gobind Singh was one of the best writers and poets that Sikhism has produced. To rectify the situation, therefore, the *Dasam Granth* was compiled some years after Guru Gobind Singh's death by Bhai Mani Singh. The *Dasam Granth* (the 'Book of the Tenth Master') was finally published in 1734.

The *Dasam Granth* is a complicated work of 1,428 pages covering many different themes. Some of the narratives in the book are autobiographical – the Vicitra Natak (Wonderful Drama), which tells of Guru Gobind Singh's background and upbringing, his time as an ascetic in the Himalayas and his life and battles with the hill rajas. There are also some poems in the mood of what has been called 'military piety' – vigorous poems in praise of God. The main part of the work, however, consists of the retelling of various Hindu legends, particularly those concerned with the goddess Chandi and the god Krishna.

The *Dasam Granth* contains one poem, the Jap (Meditation), which plays an important part in the daily meditation pattern of most Sikhs. You can find an extract from this poem below. As this extract shows, Guru Gobind Singh found it very difficult to say anything 'positive' about God, preferring to describe what God was not. The same point is made in one of the other extracts, which also comes from the *Dasam Granth*. Here all worshippers are encouraged to worship God alone and not any God-made object. This has always been a dominant message of Sikhism.

Key question What are the main themes of the *Dasam Granth*, and how might these inspire members of the Sikh community?

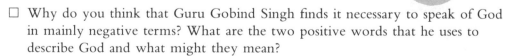

From the *Dasam Granth*:

> God has no marks or symbols, no colour or caste, not even family lineage.
> God's form, hue, shape and dress can be described by no one.
> God is immovable and self-existent.
> God shines in no borrowed splendour.
> No one can measure God's might.

☐ Why do you think that Guru Gobind Singh finds it necessary to speak of God in mainly negative terms? What are the two positive words that he uses to describe God and what might they mean?

Work to do

1. (a) Why do you think that Guru Gobind Singh did not include any of his own poems in the *Guru Granth Sahib*?

   (b) What was the main reason for Bhai Mani Singh putting together the *Dasam Granth*?

2. Here are two sayings by Guru Gobind Singh which are recorded in the *Dasam Granth*:

   ☐ *The divine Guru [God] sent me for righteousness sake. For this purpose I was born; to advance righteousness, set free the good who are oppressed, and destroy evil-doers.*

   ☐ *Recognise all humanity as one. The same Lord is creator and nourisher of all. Recognise no distinction among them.*

   (a) Try to explain, in your own words, the three reasons given by Guru Gobind Singh for his own birth.

   (b) Can you find out why Guru Gobind Singh stressed that all humanity was one? To answer this fully, you will need to look into Hinduism, which was one of the religions out of which Sikhism first sprang.

3. These are words from the *Dasam Granth*:

   Worship none but God. Do not worship things made by God. Know that God is the one who was from the beginning, the unborn, the invincible, the indestructible.

   How can the worshipper know the difference between God and the things that God has made?

13. WHAT DO SIKHS BELIEVE?

13.1 What do Sikhs believe about God?

Focusing questions
- In what different ways do Sikhs raise their awareness of God?
- What is simran?
- How can Sikhs achieve simran?

A Sikh's belief in God underlies his whole life. Yet, as his holy scriptures continually teach, no one can reach a complete understanding of God or His creation. Sikhs believe that each religion brings its own insights and approaches to God. As Guru Gobind Singh once said:

> *Men, according to different understandings, have given different descriptions of thee, O Lord.*

Sikhs believe that God is already present in nature and creation. It is the work of holy men and saints to make the people aware of God. In particular, as we shall see in 13.2, that was the mission of the different Gurus who were sent to transmit God's word to others. We have their revelations and insights preserved in the *Guru Granth Sahib* and it is this holy book, above everything else, that forms the basis of all Sikh belief and teaching.

The Oneness of God

The early followers of Guru Nanak came from a Hindu background. They had been encouraged to worship many gods and goddesses, as well as believing in the one Universal Spirit. From the Guru they learned that there is but one God and that only that God can be worshipped.

God is everything

God is everything to the Sikh. His qualities are endless, and all goodness, mercy and love are contained in Him. He has created all things. He is above all things. He is all-powerful and nothing happens without His permission. He sees into all things and directs the affairs of His children. He listens to their prayers and gives to them all good gifts. God can be reached by all people and each person's soul is part of God.

God's name

The most important religious activity for every Sikh is simran – the calling to mind and the keeping in mind of the divine name. To keep God's name constantly before them Sikhs must apply their minds constantly to those different attributes by which God is known to mankind. Yet, at the same time, it must always be remembered that God's attributes are too numerous and great for the human mind to fully comprehend.

One way for Sikhs to keep their minds regularly centred on God is by learning the scriptures off by heart, since they are so full of God's glory. The divine remembrance can also be achieved by the repetition of one particular name, Waheguru – Wonderful Lord. Simply repeating this name, however, is not enough by itself, unless the repetition involves the person's heart and soul. As the person repeats 'Waheguru' their soul is drawn closer to God and they have taken the first step along the road to salvation and peace.

Key question   **What do Sikhs believe about God?**

Extracts from the *Guru Granth Sahib*

(a) *You are clearly present in the world, O Lord,*
    Because all crave your name.

(b) *The True One was in the beginning*
    The True One was before all ages began
    The True One is, also
    Nanak says, the True One ever shall be.

(c) *No one knows the state and extent of God.*

(d) *God alone knows how great He is.*

(e) *God is the creator. He himself is invisible, but He is ever visible through His nature.*

(f) *He is behind creation and does not sit apart from it. He is immanent in every form of life. God is hidden in every heart and every heart is illumined by Him.*

☐ What do the extracts from the *Guru Granth Sahib* tell you about the way Sikhs understand God?

Work to do

1. The quotations on this page stress the 'otherness' of God. Yet the Sikh also believes that God is present in the world, as these two quotations show:

☐ ***God is hidden in every heart and every heart is illumined by Him.***

☐ ***The True One is not far from us, but resides within us.***

(a) Does the first quotation suggest that the truth of God is only to be found in those who follow the Gurus' teachings?

(b) What evidence is there in these two quotations that Sikhs believe in only one God?

(c) What do you think that the second quotation means when it says that God 'resides within us'?

2. Write a description, in not more than 150 words, of the Sikh understanding of God. Make particular use of the extracts that appear in this section.

13.2 What do Sikhs believe about the Gurus?

Focusing questions

- What linked together all of the ten Gurus and how has it been preserved since?
- What is 'enlightenment' and who can experience it?
- What has the role of each Guru been since they were enlightened?

In the early writings of the Gurus God Himself was the Guru. You can find evidence of this belief in the words of Guru Nanak quoted opposite. Later, the belief developed that by submitting himself to God in total obedience, Guru Nanak had reached 'enlightenment'. When this happened Guru Nanak, like other Gurus after him, became the vehicle for the voice of God. Later it was believed that there was a unity between all Gurus. Whilst the form varied from Guru to Guru, the spirit which linked them all together remained. This spirit passed from Guru to Guru and then into the Sikh holy book, the *Guru Granth Sahib*.

The work of the Gurus

The most important thing about the Gurus was that they had all reached the state of enlightenment. Although it is only in the case of Guru Nanak that we have a record of the Guru's enlightenment, several Gurus have left us their own descriptions of the event and their feelings afterwards. These words, for instance, come from Guru Ram Das:

> *My soul is ecstatic on hearing my Lord's coming. Sing songs of rejoicing, my friends, to welcome my spouse. My house has become my Lord's mansion.*

Guru Arjan also speaks of God as his 'spouse':

> *Blessed, blessed is my destiny, my spouse has come into my home.*

In the *Dasam Granth* these words of Guru Gobind Singh are recorded, but they could have come from any of the Gurus:

> *What he [God] spoke, that I speak.*

In other words, the message of the Gurus was not human in origin but came directly from God. God's word came to them first and they faithfully passed it on to the people. They were only God's channel. As the *Guru Granth Sahib* says:

> *The true Guru is the Word. The Word is the true Guru: that shows the path of liberation.*

Elsewhere the *Guru Granth Sahib* puts it another way by describing each Guru as simply 'the ladder, the boat, the raft by means of which one attains to God', so throwing the burden of responsibility back upon those who listen to their words. Each person must make their own response to the teachings and the example that they have been given. There is no reason why those who respond fully should not become as enlightened as the Guru since as Guru Ram Das said:

> *The Guru is in the Sikh, the Sikh in the Guru,*
> *For both promote devotion to God.*

Key question   What is the importance of the Gurus to the Sikh faith?

124

These three extracts are recorded in the *Guru Granth Sahib*.

(a) Guru Nanak

Creating all, O God, thou art the supreme Guru. I am devoted to thee and bow before thy feet.

(b) Guru Ram Das

My Guru is eternal. He is neither born nor dies.

(c) Guru Gobind Singh

Listen, the eternal God, the Lord is my Guru.

☐ Why does Guru Nanak describe God as the supreme Guru?

☐ Why do you think that both extracts (b) and (c) describe God as eternal?

Work to do

This picture is of Guru Amar Das.

(a) Who was Guru Amar Das?

(b) What clues are there in the picture to suggest that he was a holy man?

13.3 What do Sikhs believe about prayer?

Focusing questions
- How might Sikhs pray if they lead very busy lives?
- What is the Japji?
- What prayer is used to end the day and why is it important?
- What prayer forms the most important part of a service in a gurdwara?

Prayer is a very important part of religious faith in Sikhism. Those Sikhs who are members of the Khalsa make a promise to say certain prayers each day, but every Sikh tries to set aside some time during the day to pray and think about God.

Prayer in the home

Sikhs living outside India may find it difficult to make time to pray regularly – especially early in the morning. They try, therefore, to pray whilst they are doing something else, such as preparing breakfast or travelling to work.

A mother and son pray before eating

The time spent praying also varies. Some Sikhs find time to recite the whole of the morning prayer (Japji, see 12.1) with its 38 verses, either by heart or reading from the *Gutka*. Other people in a hurry may just recite the first five verses or simply recite the word 'Waheguru' meaning 'Wonderful Lord'. Whatever prayers are used, all Sikhs begin the day by reminding themselves that there is only one all-powerful God who should be worshipped. In the first words of the Japji: 'In the beginning there was truth'. At the end of the day Sikhs often recite the **Rahiras**, or listen to it being recited. This prayer thanks God for the successes of the day and so reminds the worshipper that all true success in this life comes from God alone. The prayer addresses God as 'You the Giver. You the Receiver.'

Praying in the gurdwara

Apart from praying at home, a Sikh also joins in prayers with others in the gurdwara. A visit can be made to the gurdwara on any day, but Sikhs usually meet as a congregation on the same day as most people go to worship in the country in which they live. So Sikhs in Britain, for example, meet together in the gurdwara on Sundays.

The service opens with the singing of 'Asa da Vaar' with the granthi often singing on his own. Then, towards the end of the service, the congregation sing Anand Sahib, which is a hymn composed by Guru Amar Das describing the joy that the believer feels when he or she finds God. This is followed by the most important prayer, the Ardas, when the whole congregation stands. This prayer asks everyone present to remember God and the Gurus, and to think of those who have died for the Sikh faith. It asks God to keep all Sikhs faithful to Him and to bless the whole world. At the end of the prayer, the words: 'Waheguru ji khalsa, Waheguru ji ki fateh' are said. This means 'The Khalsa belongs to God, victory belongs to God.' The same words are also used on other special occasions, such as weddings.

Key question   How important is prayer in the everyday life of a Sikh?

These two quotations about prayer come from the *Guru Granth Sahib*:

Forgetting God even for an instant is a great affliction of the mind.

Call upon God with every breath, who has made you high in the range of creation. This invaluable stage of existence is attained through grace. You must offer all your love.

☐ How do you think that someone could possibly live their life without forgetting God 'for an instant'?

☐ What do you think the phrase 'who has made you high in the range of creation' means?

☐ What is 'this invaluable stage of existence' and how is it reached?

Work to do

1. **In the photograph opposite you can see Sikhs praying before a meal.**
   (a) At what other times of day is a Sikh likely to pray?
   (b) What prayers are often used by Sikhs at the beginning and end of each day?
   (c) How do these prayers remind them about God?

2. **One line of the Kirtan Sohilla reminds the whole family:**
   Days and nights are running out of your life.
   What do you think this means?

Key words   *Gutka*: book containing hymns from the *Guru Granth Sahib*
Rahiras: Sikh prayer which ends the day and thanks God for all the successes and blessings that have been enjoyed

13.4 What do Sikhs believe about the goal of life?

Focusing questions
- What is the true purpose of life for every Sikh?
- What is 'maya'?
- What is the divine spark?

Sikhism teaches that the human soul is part of God. Most human beings, however, are totally unaware that they have the divine spark within them. This is why Guru Nanak taught his followers that the purpose of life is to encourage human beings to appreciate their relationship with the Eternal Spirit (God). It is only when a person begins to remember God with love in their heart that their attitude to worldly pleasures and enjoyments changes. They are no longer attached to them as they once were.

To win God's grace a person must model his or her life on God Himself. It is, then, the grace of God which releases an individual from the cycle of birth and death so that they can be reunited with God in perfect harmony. It is this reunion which all Sikhs continually strive for.

Suffering

It is a fact of life that all human beings suffer. The *Guru Granth Sahib* teaches that such suffering has been predetermined by God:

> *From the beginning of time, pain and pleasure are written in man's fate*
> *by the Creator.*

Of course, people try hard to minimise the effects of this suffering but it has been built into the very nature of life itself by the Creator.

Sikhs believe that, although the world is real, the way it appears to people prevents them from seeing God in it. Thus the real world creates in people's minds an illusion. This phenomenon is called 'maya' and is seen as the cause of all suffering.

Suffering, then, is seen to stem from two sources:

☐ a person's failure to appreciate God's creation or their decision to ignore it;
☐ a person's failure to control the mind, which allows it to be set on worldly pleasures and self-indulgence.

Either way the result is the same. An endless chain of actions just leads people further and further away from God. The further away that people are from God, the more their actions will be selfish. The more selfish they are, the more they will suffer.

The divine spark

Life on this earth is a testing ground for the human spirit. Having been given a soul, a spark of the divine, people start out innocent and sinless. Yet experience, knowledge and wisdom can only be gained by hard work and a dedicated life. Just as steel comes out of the furnace tempered and hard, so the soul, after a good life, comes out ready to face its final task. Through the various ups and downs of life it is the soul that leads people on the path of goodness towards their final goal. It may take one lifetime or many for the soul to reach this goal. Yet people should always be hopeful. The Creator God does not forsake those that He has made. He is constantly working to make their final salvation possible. Guru Nanak and his successors worked hard to help the people to understand this.

Key question **What does the Sikh religion teach about suffering and the goal of life?**

1. The Sukhmani (the Psalm of Peace) says:

   The Lord of man and beast is working in all; His presence is scattered everywhere; there is none else to be seen. One talks, another listens. God is in both. He is the Unity and Himself the Diversity.

   ☐ Where is God to be found?
   ☐ What do you think the phrase 'He is the Unity and Himself the Diversity' means?

2. This quotation comes from the *Guru Granth Sahib*:

   Whomsoever He chooses He unites with Himself:
   And the chosen one applies himself to His love and sings His praises;
   He comes to believe in Him with hearty faith.
   And knows that all action proceeds from the One alone.

   ☐ What does God do for those that he chooses?
   ☐ What does the chosen one do?

Work to do

1. Answer each of these questions in your own words:
   (a) What lives inside every human being?
   (b) What did Guru Nanak teach his followers about the purpose of life?
   (c) How can a person win God's grace, and what is the result?
   (d) Where does suffering come from?
   (e) What is the final goal, and how can people work towards it?

2. These words were spoken by Guru Nanak:
   Adversity is a medicine and comfort a disease, because
   in comfort there is no yearning for God.
   What does this quotation have to say about:
   (a) adversity and suffering;
   (b) attachment and earthly comforts?

13.5 What do Sikhs believe about work and serving others?

Focusing questions

- Why is it important for a person to work?
- What is the attitude of Sikhism towards wealth?
- What amount of money are Sikhs expected to give away and how is this money used?

Whilst the main responsibility for a Sikh is to worship God daily, his religion places a considerable emphasis upon the importance of work. Unless it is out of the question, every Sikh man works. A Sikh is not allowed to beg, or live off the earnings of others. The same applies to those who want to devote themselves to prayer and meditation. They cannot escape the demands made on them by the holy scriptures to work and provide for others. There is no place in Sikhism for those who would live off the goodness of others, for whatever reason.

Serving others

So long as it is honest, the kind of work that a Sikh does is not important. No shame should be attached to carrying out even the most menial of tasks. The only shame attached to work is felt by those who are earning their money from immoral or illegal activities – dealing in harmful substances such as drugs or alcohol, for instance, or misusing the gift of sex, through prostitution. The person who earns money in such ways deserves to be shunned by the Sikh community. They are dishonouring God.

Sikhs working together on a building project

So, too, is the person who believes that money is an end in itself. There is no comfort in the Sikh scriptures for anyone who devotes his or her life to amassing great wealth for its own sake. Money is only useful for buying the basic necessities of life – clothing, shelter, food – possession of money endangers a person's soul. Also in danger are those people who amass wealth by depriving others of the basic necessities of life. Guru Nanak called such people 'bloodsuckers', who could never be pure in mind or spirit.

Indeed those people who have been given a great share of the world's wealth by God carry an awesome responsibility. God expects them to use as much of their wealth as possible to help the poor and the needy in the world. To do this, they must make great personal sacrifices. As the *Guru Granth Sahib* reminds them:

> *God's bounty belongs to all but in this world it is not shared justly.*

To help Sikhs appreciate the importance of sharing and sacrificing, Guru Nanak taught them that they should give a tenth of their wealth (**daswandh**) to those who are in need. This money can be used in many ways to help the community:

- ☐ In Sikh countries where there is no welfare state, such as India or Thailand, hospitals, schools and community centres are built. These institutions are open to all people, irrespective of their religion.
- ☐ In many areas orphanages and homes for handicapped children have been established with Sikh money.
- ☐ In other areas money is provided for vital medical work. Often this includes facilities for such operations as curing blindness and fitting artificial limbs.
- ☐ Gurdwaras often have lodging houses (sarais) attached to them where weary travellers can find refreshment on their journeys.

Key question **What does Sikhism teach about serving others?**

Work to do

1. Here are two quotations from the *Guru Granth Sahib* about wealth and its dangers:
- ☐ *He alone has found the right way who eats what he earns through toil and shares his earnings with the needy.*
- ☐ *He who has more is worn by care. He who has less wanders about in search of more. He alone is in peace who has neither too much or too little.*

   (a) Can you give two examples of how the first quotation might be applied to modern life?

   (b) Do you agree with the second quotation? What are some of the 'dangers' of having too much wealth? Why do you think that it is the person who has enough who finds peace?

2. Read this quotation from the *Guru Granth Sahib* carefully:
   If we want to get a seat in the court of God, we should dedicate ourselves in this world to the service of the people.

   (a) What do you think this quotation means?

   (b) How might a Sikh dedicate himself or herself to the 'service of the people'?

Key words   **daswandh:** a tenth of a person's wealth and income, to be given to people in need

13.6 What do Sikhs believe about reincarnation

Focusing questions
- **What is reincarnation?**
- **What does Sikhism teach about the soul?**

Whilst Guru Nanak was very sympathetic to many of the teachings of Islam, he could not accept its view of life after death. Instead he followed the general teaching of Hinduism that many successive lives on this earth are necessary before a person is fit for the after-life. This belief is called **reincarnation**.

The idea of reincarnation

It is the teaching of Sikhism that a person's soul is a minute part of the Eternal Soul or God. The soul has existed since the time of creation and is waiting to be reabsorbed into the Eternal Soul. In the meantime it has a separate existence and lives through a whole succession of births, deaths and rebirths. The human soul has evolved from the most primitive forms of life before finally reaching the highest possible state of existence. This is the point from which it hopes finally to achieve reunion with God. As Guru Arjan says:

> *Since you have now acquired this human frame,*
> *This is your opportunity to become one with God;*
> *All other labours are of no use;*
> *Seek the company of the holy and glorify God's Name.*

Human inequality

The Guru was very concerned about the poor and the outcasts in society. He believed firmly that God is available to everyone and that this includes rich and poor, beggars and rulers, men and women in every society. In God's sight they are all equal. The inequality which is a fact of everyday experience is brought about by human behaviour, although the circumstances in which a person finds himself will be decided by the person's behaviour (good or bad) in previous lives.

A person's lot in life, then, is of his or her own making. Yet, if a person is born into poor circumstances, they have to improve their lot. As we saw in 13.5 Guru Nanak denounced those who were idlers and parasites and those who waited around for other people to help them.

It was at this point that Guru Nanak differed most markedly from the teachings of Hinduism. That religion taught that everyone must remain, in this life, in the caste or class into which they have been born (see 1.3). If they are to achieve a better position in life they will have to wait for another rebirth. Guru Nanak opposed this by teaching that since every person has dignity in God's sight they must be able to change their religion and occupation.

The snake and its skin

To the Sikh, heaven and hell are not future places of judgement. If they exist, then they exist here and now. Birth and death are changes in the course of life. As a snake casts off its old skin, so the soul leaves the old body at death and takes on a new one. Fortunately the soul leaves behind its old guilt and regret and so has the chance of moving a little closer to the Eternal Spirit.

Key question **What do Sikhs believe about reincarnation and life after death?**

This quotation comes from the Japji:

By His writ some have pleasure, others pain,
By His grace some are saved,
Others doomed to die relive and die again;
His will encompasseth all, there be none beside,
O Nanak, he who knows, hath no ego and no pride.

☐ What does this extract have to say about this life and life after death?

Work to do

1. In what ways do you think a belief in reincarnation might:
   (a) affect the way a person lives in this life?
   (b) affect the way that a person thinks about their own death and the death of someone close to them?
   (c) affect the way that other members of the Sikh community live?

2. The *Guru Granth Sahib* speaks about the jiva (soul, or life principle) and its many rebirths:

   The jiva was born several times as a worm and a flying insect.
   It was born several times as an elephant, a fish and a deer.
   It was born several times as a bird and a snake.
   It was born several times as a horse and a yoked bull.
   Meet the Lord, this is the opportune time.
   After a very long time you have come in this body.
   It was born several times as a stone and a mountain.
   It was born several times as the lowest life forms.
   It was born several times as plants.

   Apart from the Sikh scriptures and other religious writings can you think of any facts of experience which might lead a person to believe in reincarnation?

Key words **reincarnation:** passing of the soul into another body after death

14. SIKH LIFE AND WORSHIP

14.1 The gurdwara

Focusing questions
■ Which symbols can be seen outside every gurdwara?
■ Why is the Sikh flag an important piece of symbolism?
■ What is the focal point in the diwan and how do the worshippers show their respect for it?

The gurdwara is the building where Sikhs come to present themselves before God and his Guru on earth, the *Guru Granth Sahib*. Sikh teaching indicates that any building in which the *Guru Granth Sahib* is located becomes a gurdwara. Conversely, an act of true worship cannot take place in any building which does not have the *Guru Granth Sahib* present.

Outside a gurdwara

A gurdwara can always be recognised by the flagstaff with the yellow flag of Sikhism – the nishan sahib – flying from it. The two-edged sword (**khanda**) on the flag represents the belief that Sikhs may be called upon to struggle with both the physical and spiritual enemies of the faith. The two **kirpans** stand for the authority of the Gurus, and the circle represents the unity of God.

Apart from containing some important Sikh symbols, the flag is also a statement of a Sikh presence in the community. In the past the flag announced to a traveller, whether Sikh or not, that hospitality and shelter were close at hand. Now it is a symbol of the freedom to worship that the particular Sikh community enjoys.

Written outside some gurdwaras in Gurmukhi (see 11.3) is the inscription 'ik oankar' (God is One). This expresses one of the most important elements of Sikh belief.

Inside a gurdwara

Once a Sikh worshipper crosses the threshold of a gurdwara and enters the building, he or she is treading on holy ground. To symbolise this, the head is always covered (men with their turban and women with a silk scarf) and shoes are taken off.

The main room inside the gurdwara is the **diwan** where the *Guru Granth Sahib* is installed. The holy book is placed on cushions and covered by a canopy. When it is not being read it is covered by a silk cloth called a **romalla**. Its elevated position is a reminder that the ten Gurus also taught their followers from a similarly elevated position.

Apart from the *Guru Granth Sahib* the diwan is bare. There are no images and no seats. The people attending a service sit cross-legged on the floor to exemplify the Gurus' teaching that all are equal in God's sight and under the authority of the *Guru Granth Sahib*. During worship the sexes sit separately, with each person making sure that they do not turn their backs on the *Guru Granth Sahib* at any time.

Key question What is the significance of the symbols seen outside a gurdwara? What is the symbolic meaning of practices inside a Sikh gurdwara?

134

Flag being erected outside a gurdwara

Work to do

1. Here are some words which have been used in this section. Write down an explanation of what they mean in not more than two sentences.

   (a) gurdwara

   (b) diwan

   (c) khanda

   (d) kirpan

2. The photograph shows a flag being hoisted outside a gurdwara. Can you explain why:

   (a) there is always a flag flying outside a Sikh gurdwara;

   (b) people take their shoes off as they enter a gurdwara;

   (c) the *Guru Granth Sahib* has to be present before a building can be called a gurdwara;

   (d) the people sit cross-legged on the floor in the gurdwara;

   (e) people always sit below the *Guru Granth Sahib*?

Key words   **diwan:** literally 'royal court'; hall in the gurdwara where the *Guru Granth Sahib* is placed

khanda: symbolic double-edged sword, representing power and divinity, which plays an important part in the Sikh amrit ceremony (see 16.2)

kirpan: short sword carried by members of the Khalsa to symbolise their opposition to evil

romalla: silk covering kept over the *Guru Granth Sahib*

14.2 Worship in the gurdwara

Focusing questions

■ Why is the service of worship in the gurdwara so important to Sikhs?
■ How does a Sikh hope to receive guidance from God?
■ What is the central element in the Sikh service of worship?
■ How do Sikh acts of worship finish?

Sikhs do not keep any special day holy. The worshippers come together at the most convenient time in the week. In Britain that is usually a Sunday, although many Sikhs visit a gurdwara to pray before the *Guru Granth Sahib* at other times during the week.

A service in the gurdwara

Before visiting a gurdwara to pray, whether in the morning or the evening, a Sikh must bathe. On entering the gurdwara worshippers touch the flagpole, touch the step and then with the same hand, touch their forehead. This is in accordance with the words of the *Guru Granth Sahib:*

Wherever my Sat Guru goes and sits, that place is beautiful, O Lord King. The guru's disciples seek that place and take and apply its dust to their foreheads.

A Sikh service in a gurdwara lasts for several hours. Members of the congregation can come and go as they please, although everyone is expected to be there at the close. There are three important reasons for holding a service:

- ☐ It provides an opportunity for the worshippers to read and meditate on the words of the *Guru Granth Sahib*. Although all Sikhs are entitled to have a copy of the holy book in their own homes, many do not. Coming to the gurdwara, therefore, provides their only opportunity of studying it.
- ☐ It gives individual Sikhs the experience of worshipping together with other believers and especially of joining together in singing hymns of praise.
- ☐ It provides a practical expression of that unity and equality which are so highly prized in every Sikh community.

An important part is reached in the service when the *Guru Granth Sahib* is opened at random and a reading is given starting at the top left-hand corner of the page. This reading is given the name of **Hukam** (the will of God).

The hymns which the congregation (the **sangat**) sing together are taken from the *Guru Granth Sahib*. Many of them are thought to have been written by Guru Nanak himself.

The service ends with the Anand of Guru Amar Das, the epilogue of the Japji of Guru Nanak, a verse from a hymn by Guru Arjan and the Ardas prayer, which is said by a member of the congregation. Then there is a final Hukam which is designed to give the people a thought to take with them into the week.

The service draws to a close with the eating of the **karah parshad**. All Sikh acts of worship end in this way. This holy food is prepared before the service begins and then a kirpan is used to give the mixture a final stir as the service closes. The sweetness of the holy food is a reminder to all of the goodness of God, and its sharing with all, including non-Sikhs, shows that no one leaves God's house hungry.

After the service

Once the service has finished, everyone eats a communal meal in the langar (see 11.3). The food is strictly vegetarian and may be eaten standing or sitting – as long as everyone is doing the same. It is traditionally eaten with the right hand only. Then the *Guru Granth Sahib* is carried out of the gurdwara on the head of a member of the sangat.

Key question What are the essential components of a Sikh act of worship?

Work to do

1. The photograph opposite shows Sikh women preparing food to be eaten at the end of the service. Carry out some research of your own to discover what items of food are usually eaten in this way.

2. The word Hukam can refer to the will of God as he orders and directs the world. It can also be used for that chance reading of the *Guru Granth Sahib* which is the main way that God directs Sikhs. Do you think that these two ways of understanding the word have anything in common?

Key words **Hukam:** will of God; this is best revealed through the random reading of the *Guru Granth Sahib*

karah parshad: holy food with which many Sikh services close. It is a mixture of sugar, water, butter and semolina or plain flour

sangat: the whole Sikh congregation which has come together to worship God

14.3 The five Ks

Focusing questions

■ What is the origin of the five Ks?
■ Why is long hair an important male Sikh symbol?
■ What aspects of Sikh belief are symbolised by the steel wristlet?

We have already discovered (see 11.4) how Guru Gobind Singh formed the Khalsa brotherhood in 1699. The Guru then gave those inaugurated into the brotherhood five symbols – usually known as the five Ks. Originally these symbols had many practical uses but now their possession by a Sikh is largely symbolic.

The five Ks are very important to a Sikh because, between them, they symbolise all that he or she holds to be sacred or holy.

The kesh (uncut hair) distinguishes Sikhs from most of the other groups in northern India. **Kesh** is a sign of their dedication to God. The hair is bunched up, fixed with a comb (kangha) and then bound up within a turban. Each Sikh is responsible for keeping his own hair washed and clean.

The kirpan (sword) can be up to three feet in length or may be much shorter. It expresses the power and freedom to be found in Sikhism. Obviously it did have a practical value at one time but now it symbolises the spiritual warfare in which all members of the Khalsa are engaged. Sikhs in Britain are allowed to carry a kirpan. It is not regarded as an offensive weapon.

The kangha (comb) should be used twice a day. Sikhism places a very high degree of importance on personal hygiene: their long hair must be washed at least once every four days. The **kangha** (comb) can also be used to keep the long hair tidy underneath the turban. If the hair itself symbolises the spirituality which is at the heart of Sikhism, then the comb symbolises the discipline which is needed to keep that spirituality under control.

The kara (steel wristlet) is a steel bangle that is worn on the right wrist. The circle itself is an important Sikh symbol and it forms part of the design on a Sikh flag as well as being worn as a bracelet. It is not an ornament, but serves as a constant reminder to the wearer that: God is eternal and one; the unity which is a bond between God and the believer is eternal and unbreakable; the unity which binds one Sikh to another in brotherhood is also unbreakable.

The kachs (shorts) are trousers worn by both men and women. Hindu holy men tend to wear long cloaks and these are clearly impractical as fighting clothes. By wearing shorts a Sikh shows that he is always ready to take up arms to defend the Sikh religion. They symbolise, therefore, discipline and readiness, whilst as a modest form of dress they can be taken to indicate a sexual discipline.

The five Ks are items worn by Sikhs as external signs and some are more popular than others. Quite a few people, for example, wear a kara though they do not bother with the other symbols. For many Sikh men, though, the turban has become the most important symbol of their Sikh identity.

Key question   What are the five Ks and what do they symbolise?

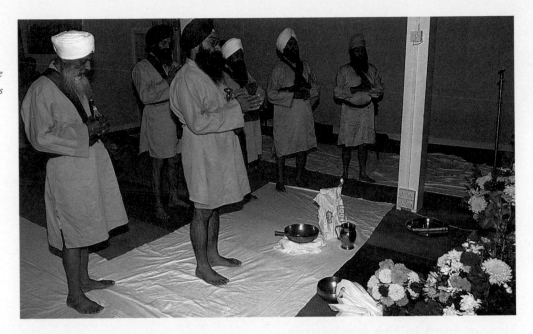

Sikhs wearing the five Ks

One Sikh writer has written this about the importance of the five Ks:

> *Eliminate symbols my Sikhlings and watch the Khalsa crumble. Take off your turban, cut the hair or throw aside the Kara, I can tell you truthfully the result would be embarrassing as well as disastrous. These five symbols have held the Sikhs in united brotherhood. They serve to make a Sikh feel and act like a Sikh. They endow him with courage to accomplish feats which would otherwise be impossible for an average man. To make a long story short, the five symbols have psychological bearing on the man who wears them. They are a manifestation of the Guru eternal.*
> **(Jeane Cutler quoted in *A Brief Introduction to Sikhism*)**

☐ What are the main reasons this author gives for keeping the five Ks?

Work to do

Guru Gobind Singh had this to say in the *Dasam Granth*:

> *The purpose for which I am born is,*
> *To spread true religion and to destroy evil doers, root and branch.*
> *Blessed are those who keep God in their hearts,*
> *And sword in their hands to fight for a noble cause.*
> *When there is no other course open to man,*
> *It is but righteous to unsheath a sword.*

It has been pointed out that Guru Gobind Singh introduced a military aspect into Sikhism which had been lacking before. Which of the five Ks might have been geared to a military way of life?

Key words   **kachs:** symbolic shorts worn by members of the Khalsa
kangha: symbolic wooden comb worn by members of the Khalsa
kara: steel bangle worn by Sikhs
kesh: long hair of Sikhs which is tied in a special knot

14.4 Food and drink

Focusing questions
- Which kind of meat are Sikhs forbidden to eat?
- What is a langar and what part does it play in Sikh communal life?
- What is karah parshad?

As a general rule the most important thing about food to the Sikh is that it should have been honestly earned and should be shared with others. Beyond that, as we shall see, there are few restrictions, although meat killed according to Islamic custom is forbidden.

Meat which is forbidden

Until the late 17th century non-Muslims living under the Mogul rulers in India were compelled to eat meat which had been killed according to Muslim custom (halal). Then, as the Sikh community became stronger and more independent, urged on by the teaching of Guru Gobind Singh, it rejected the halal laws.

Special food in the gurdwaras

Many, but not all Sikhs are vegetarians. Only vegetarian food is offered in the gurdwara, so that those who do not eat meat are not embarrassed by having to refuse it.

There is a kitchen (langar) attached to all gurdwaras, from which food is served to everyone, regardless of their caste or creed. Normally in Britain the meal is served at the end of a service in the gurdwara. Anyone who wants to can pay for their meal, though this is not necessary because preparing and providing food is seen by Sikhs as an act of charity and a service to the community. Each person is free to eat as much as they like but food should not be left to go to waste.

The idea that everyone eats from the same food, without worrying about who paid for it, cooked it or served it up, is thought to break down barriers. It is also a way of sharing in the Sikh belief that all human beings are equal in the sight of God.

Karah parshad

The food served in the langar provides a proper meal. Karah parshad, however, is a special kind of food cooked and served to worshippers in the course of their religious worship. Made from plain flour or semolina, clarified butter, sugar and water, karah parshad is cooked into a thick, pudding-like consistency.

It is then served to all who are present at the service – whether Sikhs or non-Sikhs. This shows that followers of all religions are acceptable to God. They accept it with both of their hands cupped together and then eat it immediately. It should never be spilled or wasted. If someone does accidentally spill some karah parshad the correct thing to do is to pick it up from the floor and eat it.

Drink

Intoxicants, whether in the form of alcohol or drugs, are strongly forbidden to all Sikhs. Guru Nanak himself could not see any reason why a person should want to take such substances when they only weaken the brain and the body. If Sikhs do drink alcohol, they are likely to be excluded from taking any part in Sikh worship or in the running of the local gurdwara. Only after performing some menial tasks for the service of the community are they likely to be reinstated.

Key question **What is the attitude of Sikhs towards food and drink?**

Guru Nanak spoke about food on more than one occasion. Here are two quotations recorded in the *Guru Granth Sahib*:

> *Only fools wrangle about eating or not eating meat. They do not know what is flesh, what is vegetable and what is evil.*

> *Friend, avoid that food which harms the body or provokes evil thoughts.*

☐ Many Sikhs follow a vegetarian diet. How might these two verses from the *Guru Granth Sahib* encourage them to do so?

Work to do

1. Guru Nanak had this to say about drinking alcohol:

(a) *It makes one crazy and senseless and often leads to wickedness.*

(b) *Why should anyone who deals in the nectar of God's name develop love for mere wine?*

Three reasons are given here for a Sikh abstaining from drinking alcohol. What are they?

2. Fasting (going without food) is an important spiritual discipline in many religions. Guru Nanak, however, rejected the idea with the following words:

By practising stubborn self-torture, the body wears out.

Through fasting and penance the soul is not softened.

Nothing else equals the remembrance of God.

(a) What, according to this quotation, is the effect of fasting on the soul and on the body?

(b) What is much more important than fasting?

14.5 Important holy places

Focusing questions

■ What is the attitude of Sikhism towards pilgrimages?
■ Why do Sikhs try to visit towns which are important to their faith?
■ Which town is most important for Sikhs, and why?

Unlike some other religious leaders, Guru Nanak did not place any real importance on his followers making pilgrimages to holy places. He taught them that they were searching for a knowledge of God which is to be found through contemplation and worship. It is not associated with any particular place.

In the early days of Sikhism, though, devotees did travel to the Gurus for instruction and teaching. Rather than stay in one place and turn that place into a future place of pilgrimage, the Gurus preferred to travel around. As they did so, they took care to avoid the Hindu holy places. They taught their followers that a place only becomes holy if a Guru takes up residence there.

Why visit a holy place?

When Sikhism was born there were no less than 68 holy Hindu places of pilgrimage. Most of these were situated on the banks of rivers, streams or ponds. (This is reflected in the Sikh word for pilgrimage – **tirath**.) The early Sikh teachers, however, emphasised that simply washing in the waters of a river or stream,

The Golden Temple at Amritsar

142

however blessed it might be thought to be, actually accomplishes very little.

Instead, Sikh believers are encouraged to visit towns and places which are associated with important events in the lives of the ten Gurus. It is not an obligation for them to do so, but through making such journeys most Sikhs find their faith greatly strengthened.

The important places in Sikhism

Five gurdwaras, in particular, are considered to be very important.

Amritsar is the most important town in Sikhism because the Golden Temple is located there. Begun by the fourth Guru and completed by the fifth, the temple was built with four entrances – as a symbol to announce that all people from the four corners of the earth are welcome. It is built on a platform, 20 metres square, in the middle of a pool of water. It was only in the 19th century that the temple was rebuilt in marble and the top half covered with gold leaf.

Amritsar has a unique place in the affections of all Sikhs. This is underlined by the fact that several old hand-written copies of the *Guru Granth Sahib* are kept there. Readings from the holy book begin at dawn in the Golden Temple and continue until dusk each day.

Nankana Sahib is the place where Guru Nanak was born, although it is now in Pakistan. Its name was changed from Talwandi to commemorate the Guru and there are many gurdwaras in the town.

Patna is the town in northern India where Guru Gobind Singh was born. He was the last of the Gurus and gave to Sikhism its warrior image. Many weapons, thought to have belonged to Guru Gobind Singh, are kept in Patna.

Nander: in this southern Indian town stands the gurdwara built on the spot where Guru Gobind Singh died. A horse, thought to be descended from the Guru's own steed, is kept in the stable, and the gurdwara houses clothes believed to have been worn by the Guru himself.

Anandpur is in a valley close to the Himalaya Mountains. It is not only the place where the Khalsa was born but also where the ninth Guru, Tegh Bahadur, was cremated. This is important because this Guru was a martyr for his faith.

Key question **Which towns are most important in the Sikh faith, and why?**

From the *Guru Granth Sahib* we learn:

> *If a man goes to bathe at a place of pilgrimage with the mind of a crook and the body of a thief his exterior will, of course, be washed by bathing but his interior will become sullied twice over. He will be cleaned from without like a gourd but he will be cherishing pure poison within. The saints are good even without such ablution. The thief remains a thief even if he bathes thus at places of pilgrimage.*

☐ What point about making a pilgrimage is this extract making?

Work to do
How would you sum up the attitude of Sikhism towards pilgrimages?

Key words **tirath:** literally a place of bathing or a ford; refers to the location of most of the Hindu places of pilgrimage

15. THE SIKH FESTIVALS

15.1 Sikh festivals

Focusing questions
- What is the difference between a mela and a gurpurb?
- What are the main Sikh festivals?
- How did these festivals originate?

During the time of Guru Nanak it was normal for small groups of followers or individual believers to visit him to pay their homage or to seek some form of spiritual guidance. The third Guru, Guru Amar Das, was also happy to meet his

Sikhs in Kenya celebrating the opening of a new gurdwara

followers informally but he suggested that all Sikhs should travel to meet him on two annual occasions – during the Hindu festivals of **Baisakhi** and **Diwali**. To these two festivals the tenth Guru, Gobind Singh, added a third – the spring festival of Holi – which became known to Sikhs as **Hola Mohalla**. These three festivals in the Sikh calendar are known as melas (fairs).

The melas

It was a matter of great concern to Guru Amar Das that many of his followers were still strongly attached to their old Hindu religion. He tried to wean them away from Hinduism by giving a clear Sikh meaning to the old Hindu festivals.

The changes made to the festival of Baisakhi offer a clear example of this. The old Hindu festival became a celebration which reflected Sikh religious insights and beliefs (see 15.2). During Baisakhi Hindus brought their barley and grain to the brahmins (priests) from the crops that they were about to harvest. The Sikhs broke with this tradition, however, and made the holiday the first day of the new year, a time to give thanks and to listen to the teaching of the Gurus.

The gurpurbs

Apart from the three mela festivals, other days of celebration are held during the Sikh year. These days are called **gurpurbs** and they celebrate important events in Sikh history – especially the births and deaths of the Gurus. Most of these events are only celebrated locally. Three gurpurbs, however, are celebrated by Sikhs everywhere. These commemorate the birth of Guru Nanak, the birth of Guru Gobind Singh and the martyrdom of the fifth Guru, Guru Arjan.

Sikhs celebrate their festivals according to the lunar calendar, which is based on the movements of the moon. A month is the length of time between two full moons. As a result the dates of the festivals, with the exception of Baisakhi, vary from year to year.

Key question **What are the different kinds of festival held by Sikhs and what is the main difference between them?**

> *Work to do*
> **Copy this passage into your books and fill in the gaps as you go:**
>
> It was the _____ Guru, _____ _____
> _____, who suggested that all Sikhs should visit him on two
> occasions each year, _____ and _____. The
> _____ Guru, _____ _____ _____,
> added a third festival to the other two, _____, which became
> known to Sikhs as _____ _____. These three festivals
> are known as _____. Days celebrating the birth and death of
> the Gurus are known as _____.

Key words **Baisakhi:** April festival held by Sikhs to commemorate the founding of the Khalsa

Diwali: autumn festival of lights celebrated (for different reasons) by both Hindus and Sikhs

gurpurb: Sikh festival commemorating the birth or death of a Sikh Guru

Hola Mohalla: Spring festival which draws many Sikhs to northern India

15.2 Celebrating Baisakhi

Focusing questions

- Why was the festival of Baisakhi originally set aside for all Sikhs?
- Why is the festival of Baisakhi traditionally associated with the Khalsa brotherhood and how is this link maintained?
- Which two political events from Sikh history are also recalled during Baisakhi?

Women and children taking part in a Baisakhi procession in Britain

The festival of Baisakhi, celebrated on 13 April, is the first day of the Sikh new year. In the Punjab it falls at the time of the spring wheat harvest. World-wide it is linked in Sikh minds with the inauguration of the Khalsa by Guru Gobind Singh in 1699 (see 11.4).

The tradition of Baisakhi

Before setting off for the gurdwara to celebrate Baisakhi, a Sikh must bathe at home, in a river or in the holy tank of water that is attached to many gurdwaras. Then, from early morning until lunch-time, there is a succession of hymns, prayers and speeches to remind the Sikh community of the reasons why the Khalsa was formed in the first place.

Because of this strong link between Baisakhi and the Khalsa this is the traditional time for anyone who wants to be initiated or baptised into the brotherhood to offer themselves. The ceremony which attends this initiation is called amrit samskar and is carried out by five elders (Panj Pyare) who have themselves already been initiated. You can find out more about this important Sikh ceremony by looking at 16.2.

Another tradition on Baisakhi is to renew the flag (nishan sahib) which has been flying over the gurdwara for the past year. The cloth which is wrapped around the pole is also replaced as part of the Baisakhi celebrations.

A memorial festival

Apart from remembering the origin of the Khalsa, another event is recalled at Baisakhi. This is the occasion, in 1919, when a British general ordered his men to fire on a crowd of Sikhs who had gathered together close to the Golden Temple in Amritsar. There were 379 people left dead and more than 2,000 injured. At the time there were many Indians who were not sure whether they wanted the British to leave India. After this incident the 'British out' campaign gathered momentum. This event is remembered at Baisakhi by the making of speeches which are highly political.

Amritsar

However, in Amritsar itself a very different event is held. Since the 18th century this holy place has hosted a large animal fair. Sikhs come from many miles around the city to visit the Golden Temple, join political rallies, sell their cattle, enjoy the fun of the fair and just relax before the reaping of the spring harvest begins.

Key question   **Why is the festival of Baisakhi so important for all Sikhs?**

Guru Amar Das told the Sikhs when he assembled them together:

> *Non-Sikh festivals should not be celebrated. Even if we do observe the same day we do it in our own way.*

☐ Explain how Sikhs celebrate Baisakhi in their own way.

Work to do

1. Copy out this paragraph into your books filling in the blanks as you go:

It was _____ _____ _____'s intention to wean Sikhs off the old festivals of _____ by providing those festivals with a new meaning. The festival of _____ marks the beginning of the new year in the _____ and also the end of the spring _____. Traditionally it is the time when Sikhs come forward to offer themselves for inauguration into the _____. The ceremony for this is called _____ _____ and is carried out by five _____ (the _____ _____).

2. Carry out some research of your own to discover more about:
(a) the events of 1919 which finally persuaded many Indians to support the campaign to remove the British from India;
(b) the way that Sikhs commemorate Baisakhi in India and the differences between those celebrations and the way in which the festival is celebrated by believers in Britain.

15.3 Diwali

Focusing questions

- Why is Diwali also known as the 'festival of light'?
- What event in the life of Guru Hargobind is linked with the Diwali festival?
- What happened in 1738, and how does this link up with the festival of Diwali?

The Sikh festival of Diwali is the 'festival of light', and gurdwaras are brightly lit to celebrate the coming of light into the natural world. The lights also symbolise the inner light which directs the believer towards union with God. Gifts are exchanged and it is a time for great rejoicing. Children play a prominent part in the celebrations, whose date is fixed to coincide with the new moon which occurs at the end of October or the beginning of November.

The history of Diwali

At Diwali worshippers are reminded of two important events from Sikh history. The first was when Guru Hargobind was imprisoned in Gwalior for refusing to pay the fines that the Mogul emperor, Jehangir, had demanded. When the Emperor heard that Guru Hargobind had been put into prison, he ordered his immediate release. The Guru refused to go free, however, unless 52 other prisoners were also freed. The Emperor agreed to this on condition that each prisoner left prison holding some part of the Guru's cloak. The way out of the prison was so narrow that it was impossible for everyone to hold on to the cloak. However, long tassels were attached to the end of the cloak and all of the prisoners received their freedom.

During Diwali this story is told to the children so that they can learn that Sikhs must defend their faith and the freedom to practise it. Guru Hargobind is presented as a man of great courage (the Great Liberator) since he stood up against the tyranny of the Emperor and by doing so gained political and religious freedom for his followers.

The theme of courage under oppression is carried forward in another story associated with this festival. In 1738, Bhai Mani Singh obtained permission from the authorities to hold a large assembly of Sikhs at Amritsar, but only if a large sum of money was paid into the royal coffers. This money could not be raised since Sikhs were deterred from coming by the presence of the Mogul army. Bhai Mani Singh was arrested and threatened with death if he did not convert to Islam. He refused and was executed. Some years later many Sikhs formed themselves into an army of liberation with the result that the kingdom of Ranjit Singh was declared early in the 19th century.

Celebrating Diwali

At Diwali the Golden Temple in Amritsar is lit up and there are firework displays. Elsewhere many Sikhs place clay lamps on the doorsteps of their gurdwara or on the gateposts of their own homes. Family firework displays are often held. Some women pray for the health and long life of their husbands.

Key question What is the dominant theme of the festival of Diwali and how is it carried through the various celebrations and traditions?

148

In this interview a Sikh woman is commenting upon the celebrations that go with Diwali in her family:

In most Sikh families Diwali is very much a children's festival. Presents are given and received. Stories are told in such a way that they will appeal very much to the imaginations of the children. A lot of time is spent preparing the special firework displays which are such a feature of Diwali. Those people who have the opportunity of going to Amritsar, or those who have been in previous years, show us pictures and tell us stories about the way that the festival is celebrated in the holy city. I must say that I would love to see the Golden Temple lit up specially for the occasion.

☐ Can you think of *three* reasons why the theme of Diwali is light?

☐ Which two kinds of light form the basis of the Diwali celebrations?

☐ How do the various customs and traditions associated with Diwali underline the theme of light?

Work to do

1. 'Light' is a very important symbol during the celebration of Diwali. It is, in fact, a very important religious symbol generally.

(a) Which qualities of light make it very useful as a religious symbol?

(b) Can you think of *two* examples from a religion other than Sikhism where light is used as a symbol?

(c) Can you think of *two* other symbols taken from the natural world which are used widely as religious symbols?

2. Try to invite a Sikh family into your class to find out how they celebrate Diwali and other religious festivals. In particular, try to discover:

(a) what preparations are made before the religious festival starts;

(b) how children are involved in the celebrations of the festival;

(c) what is expected from the adults in the Sikh community during the celebrations;

(d) what religious significance the festival has for each of the members of the family;

(e) any differences there would be in the celebrations if the family were living in the Punjab.

Lighting candles for Diwali

15.4 Hola Mohalla

Focusing questions

■ Who first established the Sikh festival of Hola Mohalla and why?
■ What was the character of the early Hola Mohalla festivals?
■ Where is Hola Mohalla mainly celebrated today and in what way?

Holi is the Hindu festival held in honour of the god Krishna and marking the beginning of spring. Rather than encourage his Sikhs to take part in what he regarded as a purposeless festival, Guru Gobind Singh summoned them to Anandpur in 1680 to take part in a new festival – Hola Mohalla.

Hola Mohalla procession in the Punjab

A military festival

Guru Hargobind had already established a new standing army and his grandson, Guru Gobind Singh, decided that Hola Mohalla (meaning 'attack and be attacked') would provide the ideal opportunity for Sikhs to take part in mock battles and military exercises to show off their military prowess. During the time of Guru Gobind Singh these exercises lasted for two days, reaching their climax with an attack on a military objective led by the Guru himself.

150

From the beginning, the main emphasis in Hola Mohalla has been military, although the opportunity was also taken to lay on other Sikh cultural activities. Wrestling and archery competitions are a traditional part of the celebrations, whilst from the very beginning music and poetry have also been important. The climax in the early days was the procession led by the descendants of Guru Gobind Singh, riding their elephants.

Celebrating Hola Mohalla

Today the celebration of Hola Mohalla is mainly held in the Punjab, particularly around the town of Anandpur. After a service of inauguration a fair is opened and pilgrims are encouraged to visit local shrines and gurdwaras – especially the one which commemorates Gurditta, Guru Hargobind's son and the father of the seventh Guru. As of old, wrestling matches, archery contests and shooting competitions are held, and many of these feature traditional Sikh warriors, or **nihangs**. The traditional performance of music and poetry also demonstrates and reflects the vibrant nature of the Sikh community. The festival draws to a close with a carnival procession behind the flags of the gurdwaras.

Key question   How was the festival of Hola Mohalla given its distinctive character?

Work to do

1. Which Hindu festival was replaced by Hola Mohalla, and on whose instruction?

2. Why was Hola Mohalla given such a strong military flavour? What part did Guru Gobind Singh play in the celebrations?

3. Apart from wrestling, what other activities accompany the celebration of Hola Mohalla in Anandpur?

4. How is this military flavour retained today in the celebrations?

5. Can you find out whether Sikhs in this country celebrate Hola Mohalla and, if so, how?

Key words   **nihang:** traditional Sikh warrior who used to defend the gurdwaras

16. RITES OF PASSAGE

16.1 Child-naming

Focusing questions

- **What do Sikh parents traditionally present to the gurdwara after their child is named, and what is it used for?**
- **How is the name of a Sikh child chosen?**
- **What part does amrit play in the name-giving ceremony?**

The birth of any child, boy or girl, is welcomed into a Sikh family as a gift from God. They are given the opportunity to learn about their Sikh faith from the moment that they are born. As soon as possible after birth the father whispers the Mul Mantra into the baby's ear. A drop of honey is also placed on the baby's lips.

The naming ceremony

As soon as possible after birth, the parents take their baby to the gurdwara. They take with them the ingredients for making karah parshad, as well as the gift of a small embroidered romalla – a square of silk – which is used to cover the *Guru Granth Sahib* when it is not being read.

The ceremony at which the baby receives its name is part of a religious service which the parents join some time after it has started. At this service readings of thanksgiving are given and these include one written by Guru Arjan on the birth of his son, Hargobind. In it he thanks God for the safe delivery of his infant son, who he believes was born according to 'destiny' (the will of God). So, too, is every child born to Sikh parents.

Devout parents ask that during the naming ceremony their child should receive amrit – the nectar of life – which is made by dissolving sugar crystals in water. As the granthi stirs the nectar with a khanda he recites some holy verses and prays that the child will enjoy long life and bring much joy to his or her parents. The tip of a kirpan is then put into the liquid and used to place some of the amrit on the baby's lips.

The main part of the ceremony takes place when the granthi opens the holy book, the *Guru Granth Sahib*, at random. The first word on the left-hand page is then read to the parents. They choose a name for their baby beginning with that letter. The granthi announces the name to the congregation adding 'Singh' (lion) if the child is a boy and 'Kaur' (princess) if it is a girl.

The ceremony is now almost over. All that remains is a final reading from the scriptures, followed by the sharing of the karah parshad amongst the worshippers. Presents are exchanged and most people make a donation to help poor widows and other deserving causes.

Why is the name-giving so important?

There are three reasons why this particular ceremony is such an important part of Sikh worship:

- [ ] It is a public announcement by the parents that they accept their child as being a gift from God.
- [ ] It provides an opportunity for the mother and father to give thanks for the safe delivery of their baby.

☐ It is a means of providing the baby with a name which will carry a great deal of personal and religious significance in the future.

Key question **Why is the name–giving ceremony an important part of Sikh worship?**

The Mul Mantra

There is but one God whose name is True, the Creator, devoid of fear and enmity, immortal, unborn, self-existent, great and bountiful.
The True One was in the beginning, the True One was in the primal age,
The True One is, was, O Nanak, and the True One also shall be.

☐ The Mul Mantra makes many statements about God. What are they?

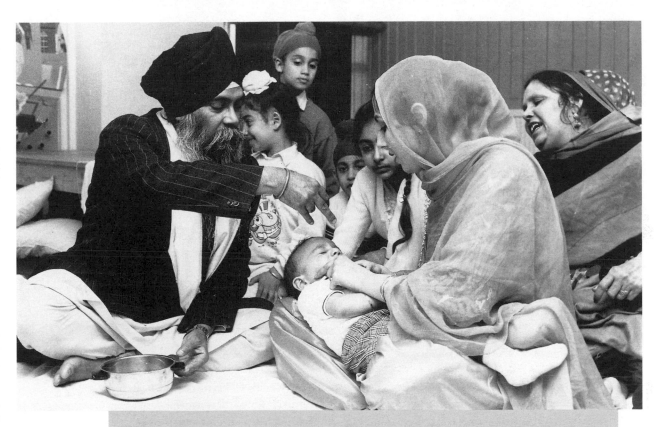

Work to do

1. This photograph shows a Sikh name-giving ceremony.
   (a) What do you think is in the bowl?
   (b) What is the man doing with it?
   (c) What seems to be the mood of the people?

2. This prayer is one that can be used during the name-giving ceremony:
   I present this child, and with thy grace,
   I administer to him (her) amrit.
   May he (she) be a true Sikh
   May he (she) devote himself (herself) to the service of
       his (her) fellows and motherland.
What does this prayer hope that the child will grow up to be?

153

16.2 Initiation into the Khalsa

Focusing questions
- What is the Khalsa?
- Who is able to become a member of the Khalsa?

An initiation into the Khalsa

When Guru Gobind Singh initiated the Khalsa in 1699 (see 11.4) he intended it to be a brotherhood of believers who would be willing to die to defend the faith from its enemies. For some time, however, the Khalsa has been a fellowship of Sikh believers who:

☐ pledge themselves to work together to uphold the truth of their faith;
☐ seek to serve the Sikh community in various practical ways.

Membership of the Khalsa is open to any Sikh, male or female, who has reached the age of responsibility and who wears the five Ks.

The Khalsa ceremony

The initiation ceremony (amrit samskar) can take place at any time, but the festival of Baisakhi is the most popular occasion. Usually it takes place in the gurdwara, although it can be conducted anywhere as long as the *Guru Granth Sahib* is present. The service is conducted by five respected members of the Khalsa (the Panj Pyare). One of these people opens the *Guru Granth Sahib*, explains the principles of the Sikh faith, and asks those who are waiting to be initiated whether they accept them.

After this a prayer is offered for the amrit (nectar) and a sixth person, acting as a granthi, reads a passage from the scriptures. Then the five members of the Khalsa kneel around an iron bowl, sugar crystals are placed with water in the bowl and a khanda (see 14.1) is used to stir the mixture. The stirring takes about two hours, during which time many verses from the scriptures are read. Finally, when the mixture is ready, the bowl is lifted up and another prayer is offered.

Each candidate then kneels before the Panj Pyare and is asked to say:

Waheguru, ji ka khalsa, sri waheguru ji ki fateh
(the khalsa is of God, the victory is to God).

Each candidate is given a small portion of amrit to drink before it is sprinkled five times on the hair and eyes. One of the Panj Pyare then tells the initiates what their future responsibilities are.

The service ends, as do all Sikh services, with the **Ardas prayer**, a random reading from the scriptures and the sharing of karah parshad, which all of the initiates eat from the same bowl.

Key question   **How are Sikhs initiated into the Khalsa?**

> ## Work to do
>
> **1. Each member of the Khalsa**
>
> | **MUST:** | **MUST NOT:** |
> |---|---|
> | set aside all other religions | cut their hair |
> | offer daily prayers | eat meat slaughtered according |
> | pay tithes (one-tenth of income) | to Muslim laws |
> | keep the five Ks | commit adultery |
> | follow the teachings of the Guru | chew or smoke tobacco |
> | | join any breakaway group of |
> | | Sikhs |
>
> **(a) Does this list remind you of any similar list in another religion? If so, which?**
>
> **(b) How do you think being a members of the Khalsa would affect the everyday life of a Sikh man or woman?**
>
> **2. Why do you think that initiation into the Khalsa is sometimes called 'a baptism by the sword'?**
>
> **3. *To fight and to accept death for a righteous cause is the privilege of the brave and truly righteous.***
>
> **How might a Sikh apply this statement today through his or her membership of the Khalsa brotherhood?**
>
> **4. Look at the photograph opposite.**
> **(a) Who is being initiated?**
> **(b) What part of the ceremony is taking place here?**
> **(c) What would the person being initiated have said to the Panj Pyare?**
> **(d) What will happen next?**

Key words   **Ardas:** formal prayer which is part of every Sikh devotional service

16.3 Marriage

Focusing questions
■ What are arranged marriages?
■ What is the symbolic meaning of the bride and bridegroom walking four times around the *Guru Granth Sahib* during the marriage service?
■ What is unique about a Sikh wedding service?

In the Sikh community marriage is not a private matter between two people. Through marriage two families become closely connected. For this reason the two people concerned have to be acceptable to each other's families, and so whole families are involved in the choice of a marriage partner. The basic conditions that have to be met before a marriage can go ahead are that:

☐ the couple must both be Sikh believers;
☐ the couple will have met and must be willing to accept each other as partners for life;
☐ the bride and groom must give their full and free consent to the wedding.

A Sikh wedding service

Anand Karaj (the 'ceremony of bliss')

It does not matter where a Sikh wedding service is held as long as the *Guru Granth Sahib* is present. In practice, though, weddings are conducted in a gurdwara in Britain. The service begins with the singing of the morning hymn, which explains just how the couple can have happiness in their future life together. The bride and groom then indicate that they are both entering into the marriage freely by bowing before the holy book.

Garlands are placed around the necks of the couple and on the *Guru Granth Sahib* by the bride's father, who takes the bridegroom's saffron scarf, passes it over his shoulder and places the end in the bride's hand. Joined together in this way the couple listen to some verses from the **Lavan**, the wedding hymn, which speaks of the love of God and the union of the self with God – a union which is now to be shown in the bond which is being effected between the man and the woman. Then, as more verses are read, the couple begin to walk slowly four times around the holy book in a clockwise direction. As they walk together flower petals are thrown over them to symbolise the fragrance of their new life together. The service ends, as do all services in the gurdwara, with the Ardas prayer, a random reading from the *Guru Granth Sahib* and the sharing of the karah parshad.

What does the Sikh wedding ceremony mean?

The journey that the couple take around the holy book is particularly important. It corresponds to the growth of God's love between the two people and the longing of the human soul for God:

☐ The first circling shows that marriage is the will of God for everyone.
☐ The second circling stirs the first feelings of love as the bride leaves her old life behind and sets off to build a new relationship with her husband.
☐ The third circling symbolises the bride's feelings of detachment from the world and her new feeling of attachment to her husband.
☐ The final circling is a reminder of the perfect love that can exist between two people.

The couple are now bound by the most serious obligations and responsibilities, as their promises have been witnessed by God, symbolised by the *Guru Granth Sahib*. No written marriage contract is necessary.

Key question **What does the Sikh wedding service symbolise to the two people being married?**

This extract from a Sikh code of conduct lays down instructions about the choice of marriage partners for Sikh children:

> *When a girl attains maturity, it is incumbent on her parents to look for a suitable match for her. It is neither desirable nor proper to marry a girl at a tender age. The daughter of a Sikh should be given in marriage to a Sikh home. If a man is a believer in Sikhism, is humble by nature and earns his bread by honest means, with him a relation may be contracted without question and with no consideration of wealth and riches.*

☐ What is it neither 'desirable nor proper' to do?
☐ Why do you think that it is desirable that 'the daughter of a Sikh should be given in marriage to a Sikh home'?
☐ What should be true of a desirable Sikh husband?

Work to do

1. One Sikh hymn includes the words:
   They are not husband and wife who have physical contact only.
   Only they are truly wedded who have one spirit in two bodies.
Explain, in your own words, what you think this means.

2. (a) What do you think the garlands placed around the necks of the groom and bride signify in the photograph opposite?
   (b) What joins the man and woman?
   (c) Who is the man standing behind the groom?

Key words   **Lavan:** hymn composed by Guru Ram Das for his daughter's wedding

16.4 Death

Focusing questions
- What do Sikhs believe about life after death?
- What is distinctive about a Sikh funeral?
- How do Sikhs mourn?

Facing death, a Sikh is comforted by readings from the holy scriptures. A favourite passage, often read in the last hours of a person's life, is Guru Arjan's Hymn of Peace.

The cremation ceremony

It would be nonsense to suggest that a Sikh does not feel death as acutely as anyone else. Great sadness is felt at the death of a loved one. Yet it is hope rather than sadness that should characterise the death of a Sikh. Death removes the last barrier that exists between God and the individual.

The cremation service is kept deliberately simple. The first act after death is for relatives to wash the dead body and then, if the person was a member of the Khalsa brotherhood, dress it in the five Ks. The body is then taken in procession to the place of cremation. The mourners sing hymns and the cortège is often followed by a band. As the funeral pyre on which the body has been placed is lit by the eldest son, the evening hymn, the Sohilla, is sung. The hymn expresses just how Sikhs feel and what they believe about life after death:

- ☐ Every person possesses a part of God which will eventually return to God.
- ☐ The soul can never die.
- ☐ By a combination of good works and religious acts of devotion the soul will eventually be reunited with God although it may need to be reborn many times before that union can be achieved.

A time of mourning

Sikhs set aside a specific time for mourning. A continual reading (Akhand Path) of the whole *Guru Granth Sahib* may take place in the 48 hours following death. If this is arranged all adult relatives take part. An alternative is to start a 'septah' (seven-day) or 'dissehra' (ten-day) reading of the *Granth* in the house of the dead person. This reading of the *Guru Granth Sahib* is called 'Sehaj Path'. Close relatives say prayers for the dead person for ten days in the gurdwara or at home. Memorials or gravestones, however, are not allowed.

Key question **What do Sikhs believe about life after death and how is this reflected in their funeral service and the mourning which follows?**

Guru Arjan's Hymn of Peace

With your eyes behold the splendour of God's presence. The company of the faithful will banish every other presence from your sight. Walk in the way of God. With every step you take you will be treading down evil inclinations. With your hands do God's work and with your ears listen to his instructions. Thus your life will be rounded off with God's approval which will be reflected in your face.

- ☐ What does this have to say about how a Sikh should live now?

☐ What does the Hymn of Peace have to say about how a Sikh should face death and what encouragement does it offer?

Work to do

1. This is the evening hymn or Sohilla:

Know the real purpose of being here and gather up the treasure under the guidance of the Guru. Make your mind God's home. If he abides with you undisturbed you will not be reborn . . . Strive to seek that for which you have come into the world and through the grace of the Guru, God will dwell in your heart.

What is reincarnation and how does this prayer refer to it?

2. (a) Why do you think that Sikhs set aside an official period of mourning?
   (b) Do you know of any other religion that does this?
   (c) What could be one advantage of such a period?

KEY WORDS

The unit number tells you where to find the explanations